Small Hotels and Inns of Andalusia

SECOND EDITION

Charming Places to Stay in Southern Spain

Guy Hunter-Watts

GW00597229

SANTANA BOOKS

Small Hotels and Inns of Andalusia
is published by:

Ediciones Santana S.L.
Apartdao 422, Fuengirola, 29640 (Málaga), Spain
Tel: 952 485 838 Fax: 952 485 367
E-mail: info@santanabooks.com
www.santanabooks.com

First published in September 2001
Second Edition – February 2004

Copyright © 2004 Guy Hunter-Watts

Design by Andrea Carter

Cover photograph by Gry Iverslin
Back cover photograph by Jane Munroe
Chapter title page photographs courtesy of the Junta de Andalucía

Map of Andalusia by Estinca Ingeniería Cartográfica

Printed by Gráficas San Pancracio S.L.,
Polígono Industrial San Luis, Calle Orotava 17, Málaga, Spain

Depósito Legal: MA-136/2004
ISBN 84-89954-30-5

This book is dedicated to my father, John Hunter-Watts.

August 2006

Dear Fi-Fi + Kieran.

- Hope you guys have many happy hol's in España, fond memoirs of Summer 06.

Love always

Clodagh + Bernard. xxx
xx
x

ACKNOWLEDGEMENTS

Paqui, my neighbour, colleague and friend, is the person that makes it all possible for me. Come rain or shine, she keeps order at my B&B, allowing me the luxury of constant sorties to visit places for this and other guide books. El Tejar wouldn't be the same without her and I owe her a thousand thanks.

Several places appear in this guide thanks to the recommendations of friends. So my gratitude to, amongst others, María José Gil Amián, Mike Llewyn, Esther Baarends, Barry Birch, Mel and Tiger, Ross and Michèle and Tikizani for putting me on the trail of some wonderful new places that have just recently opened their doors.

I am deeply indebted to Anne Cooke-Yarborough, Annie Shillito and Alastair Sawday who have helped me to find hotels and inns that offer a genuine, rather than a perfunctory welcome to their guests. They schooled me in the "special places" school and gave me my first journalistic break by leaving that fabled back door wide open.

And a final thank-you to the readers who have taken time to write to us about places that were listed in the last edition of this book. Having this second set of eyes and tastebuds was a huge help when it came to updating this second edition of the book.

CONTENTS

¡Viva Andalucía!

Andalusia continues to work its magic and capture our imaginations. Not only does it remain one of Europe's most popular holiday destinations but it is still the first choice of northern Europeans when they set up their homes in the south. It would seem that every week we read another travel article about this part of the world in our newspapers or watch another TV documentary about a couple building their dream-home in Spain.

For decades, Andalusia has had all you need if your holiday idyll is one that involves sun, sea and sand. The southern Spanish coastline, with one of the most benign climates in Europe, will always have its devotees. And the good news is that if you are heading for the beach there are more and more wonderful places to stay. The larger hotels catering for package tourists are still around but they have recently been joined by smaller, more intimate and original places. You can choose between simple but pristine hostals, funky beach-front hotels, converted farmsteads looking out to the Moroccan Rif or even a villa with the Mediterranean lapping right up to your bedroom terrace. They are all listed here.

In the last few years, inland Andalusia has also begun to attract growing numbers of visitors. Where I live in the Ronda mountains there was, until recently, just one decent place to stay—a converted millhouse that was opened with true pioneering spirit by two ex-pat Brits. A dozen years on they have been joined by many, many more places of the "small is beautiful" variety. And all of them, in their own way, offer their visitors a unique experience.

Cut through the mountains from the coast and you can now stay at desert retreats, converted monasteries, a palace that was moved brick by brick across Spain, grand town houses, isolated farmhouses, the "hi-tech" and the rustic, the flamboyant and the simple; in short, the most incredible *potpourri* of places you'll find anywhere in Europe. And the best of them are all in this book.

Their owners are both Spanish and foreign. Hospitality, of course, comes naturally to the people of southern Spain and as visitors to their hotels and rural inns you'll benefit from their natural gregariousness and generosity. Although it was never my intention to search out ex-pats when researching this book, you'll see many familiar-sounding names under "Management." I happily include non-Spaniards if they are running fantastic places and have a genuine commitment to their adopted country.

The standards of comfort in these places get better and better with each passing year, and this guide mirrors these enormous changes. In this second edition of *Small Hotels & Inns of Andalusia* you'll find almost thirty new entries, in addition to the best of those that were in the original guide (with fully up-dated information, of course). Should you choose this book as your travelling companion expect to sleep in comfort, eat superbly well and be led to some of the loveliest corners of southern Spain's sierras, valleys, villages and cities.

USING THIS GUIDE

HOTEL NUMBERS

The hotels have been numbered on a west to east basis, beginning with Huelva and ending with Almería. They are grouped by province. The hotel number on the map (see maps on pages 19-30) corresponds to the hotel number on the top of the page in the book.

ADDRESSES

Occasionally the address that appears in the book is a hotel's postal address and not that of the hotel itself. When you come to visit a place simply follow instructions in the "Getting There" section and you should have no problem finding it.

PHONE/FAX NUMBERS

Remember that some places with the same phone and fax number need to switch on the fax to receive your message. So you may have to request this first by phone. Any number beginning with a 6 is that of a mobile phone.

E-MAIL/WEB PAGES

Nearly all hotels are now using e-mail and this is often the quickest way of getting a confirmation of availability. It also makes it faster and easier for a hotel to send you further information. A hotel's web page can, of course, give you a great deal more information than we can in this guide and is always worth a quick visit, especially if you are planning a stay of several nights.

DESCRIPTION

Remember that this is my personal reaction to, and assessment of a place and it might differ in some way to yours. Please let me know if you disagree with anything or if you think that something is missing from the description. (See the form at the end of this book.)

ROOMS

We have tried to make it clear what the exact bed configuration is of any hotel. Occasionally hotels differ over what they describe as a suite. Some see it as a large bedroom with enough space for a couple of easy chairs and/or a sofa (also sometimes referred to as a "junior" suite) whilst for others the term is only used if there is a completely separate lounge. If the latter is important to you, then check at the time of booking.

PRICES

The prices we quote are those of 2004. If you are using this book after that, be prepared for a small increase. But it would be unusual for these to have gone up by more than 10%.

MEALS

Breakfast

Anyone who has lived in Spain for any length of time will know that breakfast here is often a rather meagre affair. In many hotels the standard offering is just toast and jam with coffee or tea. Fresh orange juice is becoming more common but don't automatically expect it. Be aware, too, that breakfast often doesn't get going in some places until 9am. If you need to get on the road before then, you'd be best to pay your bill the night before.

Lunch/Dinner

The price that we have quoted in the book for meals is generally that of the set menu or, occasionally when there is not one available, the average price that you'd expect to pay for a three-course meal. Be aware that waiters often don't automatically tell you what's available on the set menu, so always ask (*¿hay menú del día?*). And also be aware that dining *à la carte* can often be two or three times more expensive than going for the set meal.

We have included the dates and days of the week when some places close their restaurants, but to avoid disappointment always check, when booking, that food will be available.

DIRECTIONS

To make navigation easier its always worth having a copy of the Michelin map of Andalusia, No. 446, with you. The space we have for describing how to find any given place is limited. Many hotels will happily fax or e-mail more detailed route notes or maps for finding them. And many have detailed instructions on their web pages.

STAR RATINGS

We don't list these in this book. Personally, I've never set much store by them. There are five star hotels that have as much character as a public library and there are one star hotels that are fit for a king.

Did you know that to get that fabled fifth star you need, amongst other things, three phones in each bedroom? I can happily manage with one, or none. And how do you give a smile a star rating?

So I forgot the stars when researching this book. As a friend who runs one of the most remarkable inns in Spain told me, "the stars are in the sky."

EXPLANATION OF SYMBOLS

 Owners/staff speak English

 Hotel has room(s) with full handicapped facilities[1]

 Bedrooms have air-conditioning

 Hotel has its own swimming pool

 Pets are accepted, regardless of size[2]

 Vegetarian food can be prepared[3]

 Credit Cards are accepted

 Good walks close to the hotel

 Garden/patio area where guests can sit outside

 Hotel is suitable/caters for young children[4]

 Hotel has its own car park[5]

[1] Always check on exact handicapped facilities before arrival
[2] House rules can vary. Some hotels allow dogs in rooms, other only in purpose-built kennels. Always check.
[3] If you have special dietary requirements, let the hotel know prior to your arrival.
[4] Before you arrive check exactly what is available in the way of cots, baby-sitter, etc
[5] Some city-centre hotels' car parks aren't adjacent to the hotel so it's worth checking before you arrive.

USEFUL HOTEL INFORMATION

REGISTRATION
Spanish law still requires that you register on arrival at any hotel in Spain and they will need to see your passport or I.D. This can seem like an ordeal when you arrive after a long drive but remember that this is as tedious for hotel staff as it is for you. Once a hotel has noted down the details of your passport they have no right to keep hold of it. I would always retrieve a passport immediately so as to avoid forgetting it the next day.

LANGUAGE
Many travellers in Andalusia express amazement when they come across hotel reception and restaurant staff who speak virtually no English. Try to be tolerant of this and remember that few hotel workers in our home countries could pass the time of day in Spanish. People do try hard here but they have often not had the benefit of learning a foreign language at school. Remember, too, that a few words of Spanish, even of the pidgin variety, can go a long way.

CHILDREN
Nearly all hotels in Andalusia welcome children and find it amazing that there are places that don't. If you are travelling with very young children it is best to ring ahead and ask exactly what facilities are available; don't automatically assume that there will be cots and high chairs available. Occasionally hotels can organise baby-sitting (*servicio de canguro*) but they should be given advance warning.

BOOKING/CREDIT CARDS
Be aware that it is common practice amongst larger hotels to ask for a credit card number when you make a reservation by phone

or by e-mail. Standard practice is to charge the cost of the first night against your card. This is generally a non-refundable deposit. According to Spanish law a hotel shouldn't debit your card for more than the cost of one night for every ten booked. Some people are wary of giving card details over the phone. But you should know that to date I've never heard of a single case of fraud and that many hotels operate in this way because of the number of no-shows, particularly common with weekend tourism. When the weather turns bad, that trip to the country can suddenly seem a whole lot less attractive.

Remember, too, that many of the smaller, B&B-type places in this guide don't accept payment by credit card. We include a symbol to let you know about those that do or don't take plastic. You are rarely far away from a cash dispenser.

ARRIVAL/DEPARTURE TIMES

Some hotels have a policy of holding rooms (with or without credit card information) until a certain time – normally about 20.00h – and then letting the room if you haven't shown up by then. So if you're running late be sure to give a quick call and let the hotel know that you are still coming.

Remember that in Spain, as in other countries, most hotels require you to vacate your room by 12 noon. If you want to leave later most hotels will be happy to look after your luggage.

HEATING

Most of Andalusia's hotels have been designed primarily with keeping cool in mind. Anybody who has lived for long in southern Spain will know that winters can be wet and cold. If you're headed for one of the more simple places included here it can be well worth reminding the hotel of your estimated time of arrival and requesting that radiators be turned on before you get there. Those same marble floors that are so pleasant in summer can be an ordeal in winter. So pack a pair of thick socks or slippers.

NOISE

You are probably aware that the Spanish ear is subject to a higher decibel onslaught than any other ear in Europe. Anyone living in Spain will be familiar with the Spaniards' love of getting together in large groups and eating and drinking into the early hours. Hotels are, by nature, places where you're likely to come across people who are in party mode, and two o'clock in the morning is still early by Friday and Saturday night standards. So if you're a light sleeper, ask for a quiet room at the time of booking and be aware that many of the grander *cortijo*-style places are often used for wedding parties at weekends. If you should be given a noisy room don't feel awkward about asking to be moved.

NAVIGATING THE CITY CENTRES

Córdoba, Granada and Sevilla and some of the larger towns in Andalusia, like Arcos and Ronda, can be tricky places to negotiate when it comes to finding your hotel. It may be much less hassle to simply leave your car at any city centre car park and go to your hotel from there. All hotels charge around €15-20 for using their car park, so doing this won't be much more expensive. If the amount of luggage you are carrying makes it awkward, then it's well worth taking a taxi to your hotel. It can save you masses of time and heartache and it would be rare to clock up more than €5 in fares.

OUR CRITERIA FOR INCLUDING PLACES

When researching this guide I visited many more places than those that were eventually included. The fact that some failed to make it into these pages is no reflection of their professionalism. They were simply places at which I might not stay given other choices in the area. This is bound to be a subjective decision but I hope that I've developed an idea of what might appeal to most travellers.

You'll find hotels and B&Bs for all tastes and all budgets in this book. The bottom line for including a place is that it must be clean, friendly, comfortable and exceptional in some way or another. Just what constitutes "exceptional" can vary enormously—it might be the building itself, the views from the terrace, the peacefulness (always high on my personal check list) or the proximity to, say, the Mezquita in Córdoba or the Alhambra in Granada. Every single place that is listed here has a location that is special in some way.

Inevitably we list many more places to stay in certain areas. Take the case of the mountains round Ronda. In the last couple of years literally dozens of new hostelries have been opened. But this higher concentration reflects the simple fact that this is an area that attracts many more visitors than, say, the mountains of Jaén.

Read the text carefully and you should be able to garner why I like or have any misgivings about a particular place. There is, after all, no such thing as hotel perfection, so be tolerant of a hotel's eccentricities and individuality—you'll find no chain-hotel uniformity within these pages.

YOUR OPINIONS AND RECOMMENDATIONS

You may well have your own favourite hotel that doesn't appear in this guide. Please let us know about any place you think deserves to be included in this book and also if you feel that any of our listings doesn't match up to your expectations. With your feedback this guide will improve with each subsequent edition.

I especially welcome comments about your gastronomic experiences. When I visit a hotel I can only sample one dish and so it can be difficult to get the big picture. Please let me know of any particular hits (or misses) and also of any wines that you've really enjoyed.

Many thanks.

MAPS
SECTION

MAP 1

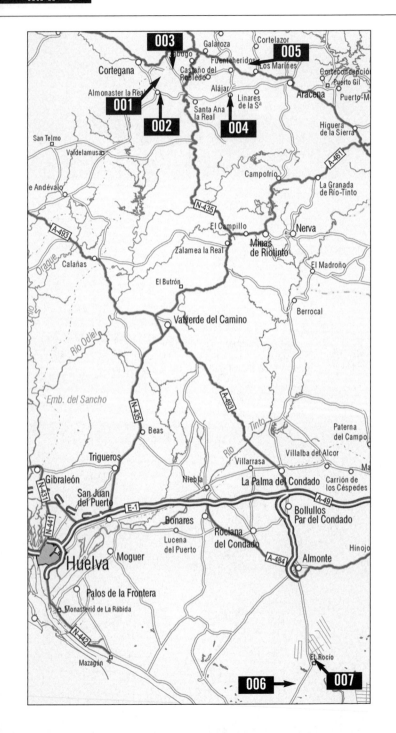

MAP 2

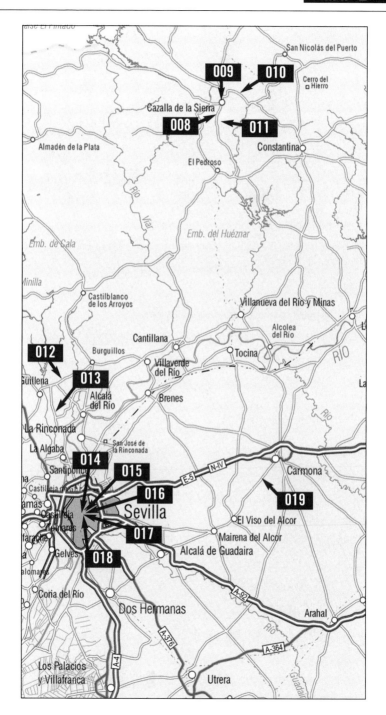

MAP 3

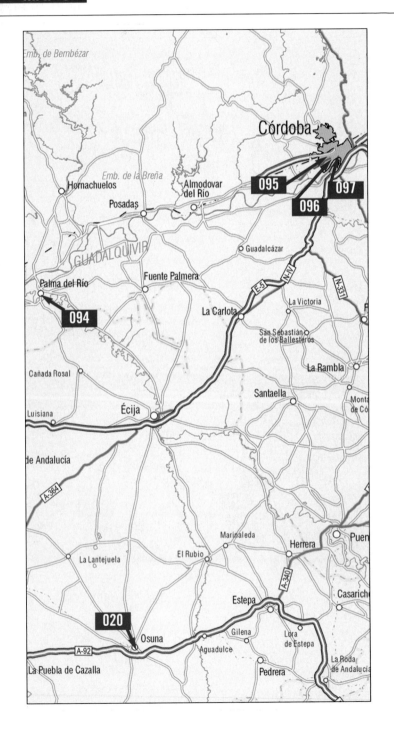

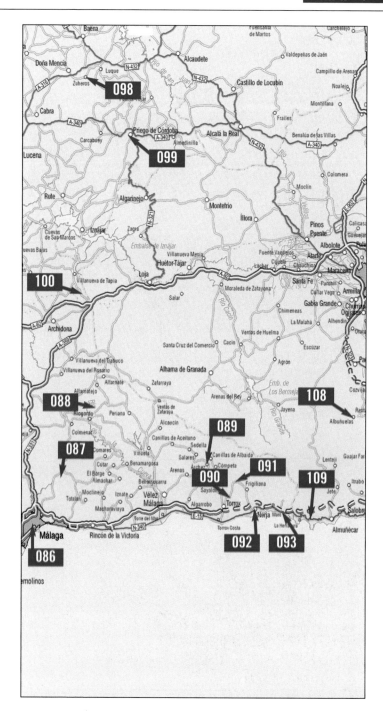

MAP 4

MAP 5

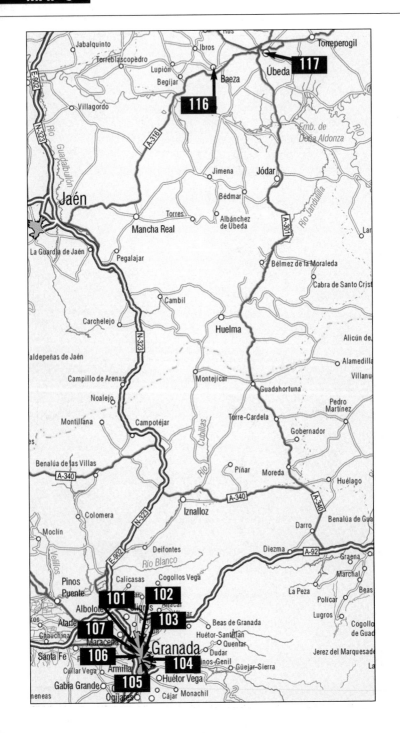

MAP 6

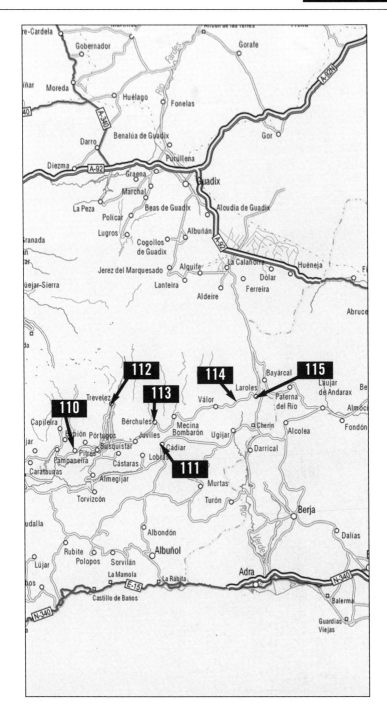

MAP 7

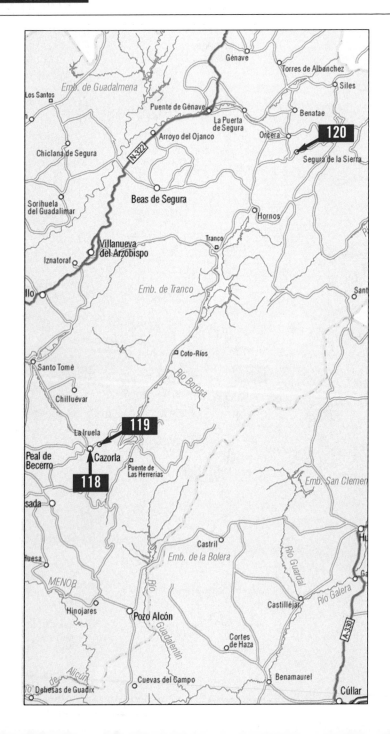

MAP 8

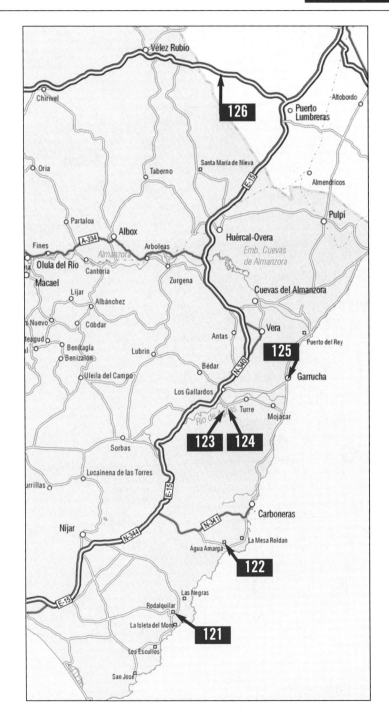

MAP 9

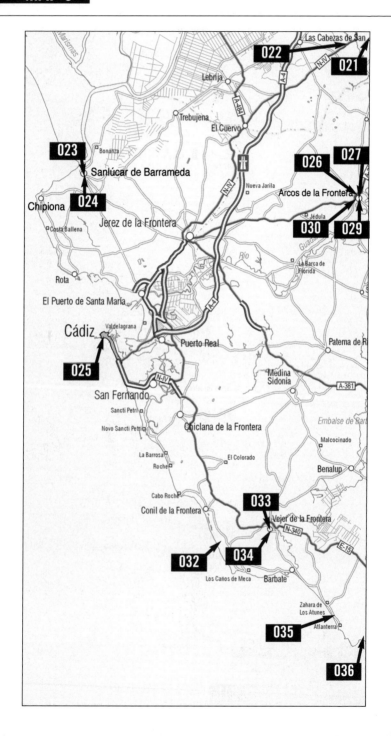

MAP 10

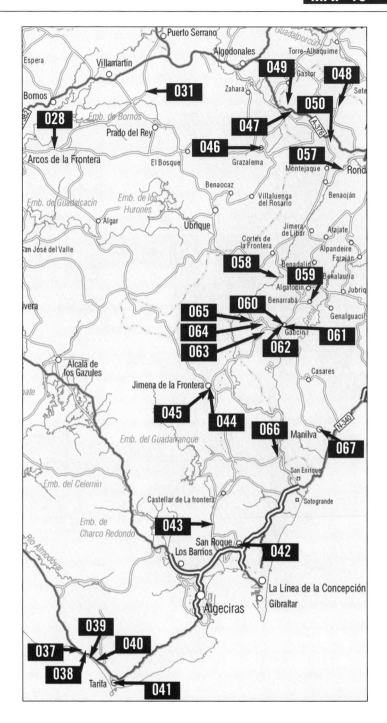

MAP 11

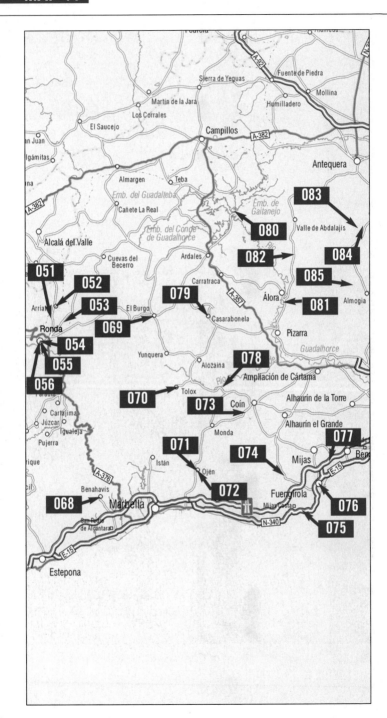

HUELVA PROVINCE

View of Cortegana

FINCA LA SILLADILLA

MAP: 1

21290 Los Romeros-Jabugo

Tel: 959 501350 or 647 913167 **Fax:** 959 501351

e-mail: silladi@telcline.es

Web Page: www.jabugo.cc

Closed: Never

Bedrooms: 1 Twin, 1 Suite, 3 Houses with 2 bedrooms and 1 House with 3 bedrooms

Price: Twin €76-89, Suite €89-108, 2 bedroomed House €152-172, 3 bedroomed House €228-267 including VAT

Meals: Breakfast included, no Lunch/Dinner available apart from snacks. Buy ingredients from the farm shop.

Getting there: From Sevilla take the N-630 north towards Mérida and then the N-433 towards Portugal. Bypass Aracena then Jabugo and turn left towards Los Romeros just past El Repilado. After 3km turn left at the sign for La Silladilla.

Management: Beatriz Iglesias Hernández

You may well have heard of Jabugo ham, the mouth-watering delicacy that has always been a favourite present to diplomats visiting Spain, adding a certain weight and sincerity to that farewell handshake at Barajas. But you probably won't have heard of Finca La Silladilla, lost as it is in a sea of cistus and oak-forest in a little-known corner of Huelva. You journey here by way of winding country lanes and a narrow stonewalled track which leads you up to the farm—a sight for the sorest of travel-weary eyes. Your room will either be in the main farmhouse or in one of two nearby cottages. The decoration and furnishings are stylish without a hint of showiness, a successful mix of bright fabrics and local base elements such as granite, terra-cotta and chestnut. Although Silladilla's young live-in staff serve only breakfast (outside in summer, in your room when temperatures fall), there's a bar doubling as a shop/delicatessen where you can buy the makings of a simple, yet gourmet, supper. Wine buffs won't believe their luck when they check the labels on the bottles—and the prices.

To see and do: visit to one of the Jabugo ham *secaderos* (drying sheds), walking in the Natural Park of Aracena, day trips to Portugal

CASA GARCÍA

MAP: 1

Avenida de San Martín 2
21350 Almonaster la Real

Tel: 959 143109 **Fax**: 959 143109

Closed: Never

Bedrooms: 3 Doubles, 18 Twins and 1 Suite

Price: Double/Twin €48, Suite €90 + 7% VAT

Meals: Breakfast €6, Lunch/Dinner €12 excluding wine

Getting there: From Aracena take the N-433 towards Portugal. Shortly before reaching Cortegana turn left to Almonaster. Casa García is on the right at the entrance to the village.

Management: Juan García Portero

Almonaster la Real is one of the loveliest of a string of mountain villages which stretch west through the Aracena Park towards the Portuguese border. Walking the old paths which link these places feels rather like re-discovering Hardy's Wessex. The García family have been feeding locals for almost three decades but it was only recently that they completely revamped a simple village eatery to create a stylish and supremely comfortable small hotel and restaurant. You arrive by way of a shady terrace, a great place from which to watch the world (and the occasional car or donkey) pass you by. On the two floors above are the bedrooms whose comfort and quality will take you by surprise given their paltry price-tag. Forego a balcony and ask for one that looks out across the prettiest of gardens to the rear of the building. Casa García's traditional Huelva cuisine is superb. Many ingredients come fresh from the village *huertas* (allotments), the pork and sausages are of the best, and the decoration, bright and fresh, is conducive to a memorable, leisurely and satisfying meal.

To see and do: visit to the Mezquita in Almonaster, day trips to Portugal, walking in the Natural Park of Aracena

FINCA LOS GALLOS

MAP: 1

Estación de Almonaster s/n
21350 Almonaster la Real

Tel: 959 501167 or 687 365754 **Fax:** 959 501167

e-mail: info@andaluciapark.com

Closed: Never

Bedrooms: 6 Cottages sleeping 2-6

Price: Cottage for 2 €54-60, Cottage for 4 €90-96,
Cottage for 6 €126-144 + 7% VAT

Meals: Breakfast €6

Getting there: From Aracena take the N-433 towards Portugal. Go through the small village of El Repilado then at km post 112 turn left towards Almonaster la Real. Los Gallos is approximately 2km further on the left.

Management: Ana Rico Castelló

Long a favourite weekend retreat for *Sevillanos* in-the-know, the Aracena Park is beginning to see more and more visitors from further afield. Most come to walk or ride the network of ancient footpaths that crisscross the area, linking some of Andalusia's prettiest villages. One of the loveliest of all is Almonaster la Real where, just to the north of the village, in a tiny hamlet, lies Los Gallos, a great base for exploring the area. The buildings making up the *finca* that was once a small factory where anis was made had lain long abandoned until Ana and her husband discovered the place. They have gradually restored and renovated, creating six simple self-catering guest houses. These are decorated with a mix of modern and antique furnishings. All of them have either a fireplace or a wood burning stove and everything you need to prepare your own meals. But the nicest thing by far about Los Gallos is its garden, an enchanting tangle of greenery made up of fig trees, vines, magnolia, loquats, willows and oaks, with its pretty, spring-fed pool beside which you can breakfast in the warmer months.

To see and do: walking, visits to the Mezquita of Almonaster and day trips to Portugal

MOLINO RÍO ALÁJAR

MAP: 1

Finca Cabeza del Molino s/n
21340 Alájar

Tel: 959 501282 **Fax:** 959 125766

e-mail: rioalajar@wanadoo.es

Web Page: www.molinorioalajar.com

Closed: Never

Bedrooms: 5 Houses sleeping 2-6

Price: House for 2 €210 for weekend or €460 for week, House for 4-6 €360 for weekend or €770 for week + 7% VAT

Meals: No meals available but a hamper with all the basics can be provided on arrival for €25-35

Getting there: From Aracena follow the signs to Alájar. Pass above Alájar on the road towards Santa Ana then turn left at signs for Ermita de San Bartolomé. Cross the bridge, then after 50m turn right and follow the narrow track to Molino Rio Alájar.

Management: Monica de Voos & Peter Jan Mulder

Ancient cobbled footpaths and bridle ways wind through the hills west of Aracena linking some of Andalusia's prettiest villages. My personal favourite is Alájar whose twisting, narrow alleyways are dominated by the lofty mountain chapel of Arias Montero. Just below the village is a converted mill, as bucolic an idyll as you could hope to find. Monica and Peter, the Dutch owners, have built five cottages just up the hillside from the original mill house in a beautiful swathe of wooded hillside. The houses exude a warmth born of their dark chestnut beams, honey-coloured walls and hand-made terracotta floor tiles. All of the cottages are large enough for you to be entirely independent but if you're feeling sociable there is a huge guest lounge in the mill house with loads of books, magazines and Peter's detailed notes for several different walks leading straight out from the farm. You can also cover the same footpaths by donkey with a local guide. Although this place is set up for self-catering, a welcome hamper of goodies can be provided and a restaurant in the village can deliver a meal directly to your cottage.

To see and do: walking and riding, visits to villages of the Sierra, day trips to Portugal and Sevilla

FINCA BUEN VINO

MAP: 1

Los Marines
21293 Aracena

Tel: 959 124034 **Fax:** 959 501029

e-mail: buenvino@facilnet.es

Web Page: www.buenvino.com

Closed: July, August and Christmas & New Year

Bedrooms: 4 Doubles and 3 Cottages with their own pools

Price: Double €140-160 + VAT (reductions for longer stays), Cottages €1000 weekly high season or from €400 weekly low season

Meals: Breakfast included, Dinner €30 excluding wine

Getting there: Bypass Aracena and the village of Los Marines and look for a sign for Buen Vino approximately 1.5km after Los Marines on the right (near the km 95 marker post).

Management: Jeannie & Sam Chesterton

"Buen Vino"—just writing the words evokes happy memories of what must be one Andalusia's most amazing country retreats. This elegant country home stands alone in a beautiful swathe of chestnut and oak forest. You feel a frisson of excitement as you approach the house along the long track. This is a home rather than a hotel. A stay with Sam and Jeannie is about enjoying a ready-made, supremely convivial house-party atmosphere. Each bedroom is different to the next, with stacks of paintings, magazines, books and individual decorative flourishes. Downstairs a cosy, panelled dining room provides the perfect stage for Jeannie's *cordon bleu* suppers. The food is fantastic, the wines superb and the Chestertons are relaxed, entertaining hosts. There's a beautiful pool tucked a discrete distance from the house and walks galore straight out from the house. Book a week's stay in one of the cottages if you are really keen to commune in comfort with nature, but remember that a car is essential to get the most out of staying here. If you enjoy cooking call Jeannie for details of the cookery courses that she organises at Buen Vino.

To see and do: visits to the Gruta de las Maravillas cave in Aracena and the villages of the Aracena Natural Park, swimming and picnics at the reservoirs

EL CORTIJO DE LOS MIMBRALES

MAP: 1

Ctra del Rocío A-483 km 20
Tel: 959 442237 **Fax:** 959 442443

e-mail: cortijomimbrales@futurnet.es

Web Page: www.cortijomimbrales.com

Closed: Never

Bedrooms: 6 Doubles, 14 Twins and 6 Cottages sleeping 2 or 4

Price: Double/Twin €125-150, Duplex Doubles €200,
Cottage for 2 €250, Cottage for 4 €350 + 7% VAT

Meals: Breakfast included, Lunch/Dinner €15-20 including wine

Getting there: From Sevilla, go west on the A-49 motorway towards
Portugal. Exit for Bolullos del Condado and follow the A-483
towards Malalascañas. The hotel is on the right, 4km past El Rocío.

Management: José Joaquín Aguirre

Anyone who has journeyed to El Rocío will know that the Doñana Park has a unique beauty, one which somehow eludes capture on film or in prose. Just a five minute drive from the larger-than-life Rocío sanctuary is one of southern Spain's most striking small hotels. The outside of this low, *hacienda*-style building (it lies at the heart of a vast citrus plantation) is already appealing but it is the brilliant use of colour that is so attractive and original. Everywhere the eye wanders you see some remarkable feature—bright colour washes, exuberant roses, ferns and jasmine, a seductive commingling of antique furnishing and contemporary design. Choose between a room or a cottage; all are four-star comfortable and have been decorated with enormous flair. The night after staying here I made a long journey back to eat a second meal in Los Mimbrales' beautiful, high-ceilinged restaurant. The combination of great food and décor, good-natured, efficient service and the pampering of all five senses make this an unforgettable experience... and there are great beaches nearby, too.

To see and do: visits to the Doñana National Park, the Sanctuary of the El Rocío Virgin, and the beaches

HOTEL TORUÑO

MAP: 1

Plaza Acebuchal 22
21750 El Rocío

Tel: 959 442626 or 959 442323 **Fax:** 959 442338

e-mail: hoteltoruno@terra.es

Web Page: www.fundaciondonana.es

Closed: Never

Bedrooms: 2 Singles, 5 Doubles and 23 Twins

Price: Single €52.50, Double/Twin €75 + 7% VAT

Meals: Breakfast included, Lunch/Dinner €14.50 including wine

Getting there: From Sevilla, go west on the A-49 motorway towards Portugal then exit for Bolullos del Condado. Follow the A-483 towards Malalascañas to El Rocío. The hotel is 200m behind the Rocío Sanctuary.

Management: Juan María Sánchez

Any estate-agent or hotelier will tell you it's all about one thing—location. And the 'L' factor comes no higher than at El Toruño. It is just a hundred metres from the shrine of the Rocío Virgin, right in the centre of the vast Doñana reserve and just metres from the lagoon which brings ornithologists flocking from all over the world. I'll never forget awakening to a blushing dawn and seeing the outline of several dozen flamingos gradually sharpen as a languid February sun burned off the early morning mist. Be sure to get a room with a view. The best, number 225, has windows on two sides and all odd-numbered rooms between 207 and 217 catch a part of that incredible *vista*. Each bedroom, fittingly, is dedicated to a different species of bird and even in the bathrooms there are hand-painted pictures of things feathered. Everything is as clean as clean can be. You eat in a sister restaurant just across the way where specialities include fish and organic beef raised in the Doñana reserve. This is a unique hotel in a unique village, which out of season, feels like a deserted Wild West town.

To see and do: visits to the Doñana National Park, the Sanctuary of El Rocío Virgin, and the beaches

SEVILLA PROVINCE

Torre del Oro

TRASIERRA

MAP: 2

Cazalla de la Sierra
41370 Cazalla de la Sierra

Tel: 954 884324 **Fax:** 954 883305

e-mail: trasierra@trasierra.net

Closed: End October - mid March

Bedrooms: 1 Single, 7 Doubles, 2 Twins and 1 Suite

Price: Single €125, Double/Twin €250, Suite €310 including VAT

Meals: Breakfast included, Lunch €24,
Dinner €36 excluding drinks

Getting there: From Sevilla airport take the SE-111 via Brenes to
Cantillana. Here take the A-432 towards Cazalla de la Sierra.
Trasierra is on the left hand side at km 44.5, shortly before you reach
Cazalla.

Management: Charlotte Scott

Just south of the sleepy mountain town of Cazalla, high in the Sierra Morena mountains and surrounded by a vast estate of chestnut and oak forests, Trasierra is unquestionably one of the most beautiful and enchanting places to stay in Andalusia. Charlotte Scott, with huge amounts of flair and creative *savoir-faire*, has created an exceptional series of spaces in this ancient *almazara* (olive mill). People come to stay here, many of them from London, in the knowledge that they will eat beneath the stars in a perfumed garden, sleep in style and great comfort, find the atmosphere of an exclusive house-party and be pampered by the bright and friendly staff. There is nothing 'ordinary' to be found at Trasierra; this is a place that nurtures dreams, may inspire you to write or to paint and where you should, to quote the literature that is waiting in your room, 'feel free to look fabulous at night'. You may arrive to the sound of Charlotte's son George playing the piano, you will probably have your candlelit dinner prepared by her daughter Giaconda and will certainly be cared for by the ever-helpful and charming manager Manolo. *Grand cru andalou!*

To see and do: Carmona and Sevilla, the towns of Constantina and Cazalla, walking and riding in the Natural Park

PALACIO DE SAN BENITO

MAP: 2

San Benito s/n
41370 Cazalla de la Sierra

Tel: 954 883336 **Fax:** 954 883162

e-mail: info@palaciodesanbenito.com

Web Page: www.palaciodesanbenito.com

Closed: Never

Bedrooms: 9 Twins and Doubles

Price: Twin/Double €120-210 + 7% VAT

Meals: Breakfast included, Lunch/Dinner €25-35 excluding wine

Getting there: From Sevilla follow the A-431 to Cantillana. Here take the A-432 via El Pedroso to Cazalla. Arriving at the junction on the south of town, go straight across and up the hill past the Posada del Moro. San Benito is on the right.

Management: Mañuel Morales de Júdar

There can be few quirkier, more remarkable places to stay in
Andalusia than San Benito. When Mañuel inherited this remarkable
building there was just one problem; it wasn't where he wanted to
live. Instead of selling he decided to move his grandmother's home,
wafer brick by wafer brick to lovely Cazalla. Then he set about
decorating it with a flair and flamboyance that must be seen to be
believed. The place has the feel of a series of stage sets with a
different mood pervading each of the rooms. Here Renaissance meets
Mudéjar, things classical with those eclectic, and 'trad' Spain
embraces the Home Countries. The result is a riot. You swim in the
fountain-fed pool of a cloistered patio, sip your pre-dinner *fino* in a
library-lounge that seems plucked from an Oscar Wilde novel, then
dine in stately splendour in an amazing dining room-cum-banquet
hall. Bedrooms are every bit as whacky, with flounces, baldequins,
Dior fabrics and bathrooms big enough to dance a waltz. There are
tapestries, statues and dozens of portraits of the owner's blue-blooded
ancestors. Surprises galore await you at San Benito—and all of them
agreeable ones.

To see and do: walking in the Sierra del Norte Natural Park,
the old centre of Cazalla de la Sierra including the church of
La Consolación and the Carthusian monastery, La Cartuja

LA CARTUJA DE CAZALLA

MAP: 2

Ctra Cazalla - Constantina A-455 km 2.5
41370 Cazalla de la Sierra

Tel: 954 884516 **Fax:** 954 884707

e-mail: cartujsv@teleline.es

Web Page: www.skill.es/cartuja

Closed: 24/25 December

Bedrooms: 2 Singles, 1 Double, 5 Twins and 4 Suites

Price: Single €55, Double/Twin €90, Suite €120 + 7% VAT

Meals: Breakfast included, Lunch/Dinner €20 including wine

Getting there: From Sevilla follow the A-431 to Cantillana and then take the A-432 via El Pedroso to Cazalla. Here follow the signs through town for Constantina. After leaving the town continue for 2.5km on the A-455 then turn left at the sign for La Cartuja.

Management: Carmen Ladrón de Guevara

There is nowhere to stay in Spain quite like La Cartuja. It is impossible to imagine what confronted Carmen de Ladrón de Guevara when some two decades back she bought this crumbling Carthusian monastery. She didn't simply hope to restore these old stones, she wanted to breathe new artistic and spiritual life into a building whose remarkable physical setting seems to lift you above the mundane and inspire you to greater things. Literally hundreds of lorry-loads of rubble were cleared away and architectural shape and structure gradually re-emerged from the dense foliage that had all but engulfed the building. You stay in one of the monk's cells or perhaps in the annex that Carmen was already hailing as 'a building for the New Millennium' several years back. The silence at night, the extraordinary church and a dinner with Carmen make for a totally unique experience. Thanks to her single-mindedness, La Cartuja has become a forum for artistic debate, a touchstone for the creative impulse, as well as an extraordinary place to stay.

To see and do: visits to the Huesnar river valley, the Arab and English mines in the Sierra del Hierro, not to mention La Cartuja itself

LAS NAVEZUELAS

MAP: 2

A-432 km 43.5, Apartado de Correos 14
41370 Cazalla de la Sierra

Tel: 954 884764 **Fax:** 954 884594

e-mail: navezuela@arrakis.es

Web Page: www.lasnavezuelas.com

Closed: 7 January - 20 February

Bedrooms: 1 Double, 3 Twins, 2 Suites, 3 Apartments for 2,
1 Apartment for 4 and 1 Apartment for 6

Price: Double/Twin €63, Suite €74, Apartment for 2 €85,
Apartment for 4 €97, Apartment for 6 €130 + 7% VAT

Meals: Breakfast included (but not for apartments), Lunch/Dinner
€17 excluding wine. In summer only lunches are served, in winter
only dinners.

Getting there: From Sevilla follow the A-431 to Cantillana. Here
take the A-432 via El Pedroso towards Cazalla. Pass the km 43
marker post, continue for 500m then turn right and follow a track to
Las Navezuelas.

Management: Luca Cicorella

Luca and his wife Miariló were already making waves at Las Navezuelas long before the phrase *turismo rural* had entered the vernacular. Thanks to their vision, this small country hotel is now considered a role model for young folk with similar aspirations. The setting is deeply bucolic—a low, whitewashed *lagar* (farm where oil was milled) with nothing except the occasional flock of sheep or goats to interrupt a sweeping panorama of farmland that stretches for kilometres and kilometres. The decoration of bedrooms and communal space is fresh, simple and rustic and the overall feel of Las Navezuelas is uncluttered and soothing, the sort of place that could inspire you to put a pen to paper or to reach for the sketch pad. The food philosophy is similar to the decorative one traditional and wholesome with no airs of grandeur. Guests return year after year and so, too, the stork that nests on a rooftop turret. Wake to birdsong, breakfast to Bach, dine to Enya. An aural as well as a visual feast awaits you here, and there are wonderful walks straight out from Las Navezuelas.

To see and do: visits to the Huesnar river valley, the Sierra del Viento for panoramic views of the Sierra, and the villages of Cazalla and El Pedroso

HOTEL CORTIJO ÁGUILA REAL

MAP: 2

Ctra Guillena-Burguillos km 4
41210 Guillena

Tel: 955 785006 **Fax:** 955 784330

e-mail: hotel@aguilareal.com

Web Page: www.aguilareal.com

Closed: Never

Bedrooms: 10 Twins and 4 Suites

Price: Twin €80-120, Standard Suite €120-170, Superior Suite €140-190 + 7% VAT

Meals: Breakfast €10, Lunch/Dinner €25 excluding wine

Getting there: From Sevilla take the N-630 towards Mérida then go right on the SE-180 to Guillena. Go through the village and at the second set of traffic-lights turn right on the SE-181 towards Burguillos. Continue straight across the roundabout. The hotel is signposted to the right after approx. 4km.

Management: Isabel Martínez

Several of the grand old *cortijos* (farms) close to Sevilla had a new lease of life breathed into them thanks to a one-off event—the extraordinary 92 Expo—that awakened the world to the narcotic charms of Andalusia. Águila Real is one of their very best, a perfect place to stay if you want to visit Sevilla yet sleep deep in the country, far from the whine of mopeds and buzz of a city that parties until past 5am. It is the quintessential Sevillian *cortijo*, sitting alone on a hill, adrift in a sea of wheat and sunflowers. Massively thick whitewashed walls wrap around a vast courtyard, where dovecot, water trough and stables remind you that this remains a working farm. Inside things are less rustic. There are antiques, bright pastel tones, an honesty bar and a mood of simple elegance. The dining room is particularly intimate and meals include a lot of home-grown produce. You certainly eat well here. Bedrooms are big with air-conditioning and a serendipitous mix of decorative styles. Choose one leading straight out to the beautiful garden from where there is an amazing view of Sevilla by night.

To see and do: visits to Sevilla, Carmona, Aracena and the Roman ruins of Itálica

CORTIJO TORRE DE LA REINA

MAP: 2

Paseo de la Alameda s/n
41209 Torre de la Reina (Guillena)

Tel: 955 780136 **Fax:** 955 780122

e-mail: info@torredelareina.com

Web Page: www.torredelareina.com

Closed: Never

Bedrooms: 6 Twins and 6 Suites

Price: Twin €109-134 Suite €146-177 + 7% VAT

Meals: Breakfast €10, Lunch/Dinner €24 excluding wine

Getting there: From Sevilla take the N-630 north towards Mérida. Shortly after passing the ruins of Itálica turn right towards Córdoba and continue to Algaba. Here, at the roundabout, take the C-341 towards Alcalá del Río and after 1.5km turn left to Torre de la Reina. The hotel is on the left as you enter the village.

Management: José María Medina Contreras

There is much history wrapped into the fabric of this beautiful old *cortijo* (farm). In the thirteenth century King Ferdinand's army camped here during the conquest of Sevilla. A century later it passed into the possession of Queen María de Molina—thus the name. Recently declared a National Monument, it is now home to one of Andalusia's most seductive small hotels. Here is the distilled romantic vision of Andalusia—layer upon layer of whitewash contrasted by thick bands of ochre, bougainvillaea, geraniums and ferns, air heavy with the scent of jasmine and orange blossom. A number of linked patios lead to a formal garden which is subtly lit at night. You can see why this place is often chosen for wedding parties. The bedrooms and suites (my personal favourite is No. 4) are also seductive spaces. There are esparto mats, old prints and oil paintings, antique wardrobes and dressers and a full complement of creature comforts. Add to this an authentically Andalusian cuisine which looks to the season for its ingredients, a gorgeous vaulted lounge and you begin to get the measure of this remarkable place.

To see and do: the city of Sevilla, Carmona, and the ruins of Itálica

CASA Nº 7

MAP: 2

Calle Virgenes 7
41004 Sevilla

Tel: 954 221581 **Fax:** 954 214527

e-mail: info@casanumero7.com

Web Page: www.casanumero7.com

Closed: Never

Bedrooms: 4 Doubles and 2 Twins

Price: Double/Twin €170 + 7% VAT

Meals: Breakfast included, no Lunch or Dinner available. There are numerous choices of bars and restaurants close to the hotel.

Getting there: Park in any city-centre car park (the nearest is 'Cano y Cueto' at the junction of Calle Cano y Cueto and Menéndez Pelayo). Then take a taxi to the hotel.

Management: Gonzalo del Río y Gonzalez-Gordon

Recently voted *Small Hotel of the Year* by the London magazine *Tatler*, there is nowhere to stay in the city quite like Casa No.7. A host of details give away a certain nostalgia for the Noel Coward era; scrambled eggs (in olive oil) at breakfast, a white-jacketed butler who whisks your suitcase up to your room, and an elegant drawing room where you will be served a glass of chilled *fino* (dry sherry) before you head out for dinner. And it will be the very best of *finos* because Gonzalo, whose family own the González-Byass *bodegas,* knows more than a thing or two about sherry! Comfort and elegance are the keynotes of the bedrooms he created at Casa No 7. Carefully chosen fabrics, rugs, antique dressers, old prints and oils, family photographs and books give them both a homely and elegant feel. Marble floors, double sinks and air-conditioning would delight the most exacting of hotel inspectors. It all feels like a privileged world-within-a-world, an inner *sanctum* safe from the heat and the rumble of the Andalusian capital. With luck you may meet Gonzalo and share conversation about changing times in the sherry trade. Like that man Jeeves, he and his hotel are inimitable.

To see and do: the Cathedral and the Giralda, the Jewish Quarter, the Plaza de España and the María Luisa Park

HOTEL SIMÓN

MAP: 2

Calle García de Vinuesa 19
41001 Sevilla

Tel: 954 226660 or 954 226669 **Fax:** 954 562241

e-mail: info@hotelsimonsevilla.com

Web Page: www.hotelsimonsevilla.com

Closed: Never

Bedrooms: 5 Singles, 8 Doubles, 11 Twins and 5 Suites

Price: Single €53, Double/Twin €86, Suite €113 + 7% VAT

Meals: Breakfast €4, no Lunch or Dinner available, but a huge choice of bars and restaurants close to hotel

Getting there: Head along the Avenida de la Constitución passing in front of the Cathedral (police will let you pass if you explain that you are heading for hotel) then turn left into Calle Vinuesa. Easier still, park in any city-centre car park (e.g., El Arenal, Plaza Nueva) and take a taxi to the hotel.

Management: Francisco Aguayo

The Hotel Simón has long been a favoured sleep-over with travellers to Sevilla. You couldn't hope to find a better-situated hotel, just metres from the largest Gothic cathedral in Europe, a shake away from the beautiful Calle Sierpes and a stone's throw from the River Guadalquivir. Francisco Aguayo has long been at the helm and this gentle-mannered *Sevillano* (he speaks excellent English) has never been one to rest on his laurels. He is constantly refurbishing and redecorating, determined not only to maintain but also to improve his hotel. A classic facade of wrought-iron *rejas* and balconies sets the tone of The Simón and its authentically Andalusian feel follows through into the columned, 18th century ceramic-tiled patio-courtyard. Potted ferns and oils, uniformed staff, gilt mirrors and oil paintings all have a slightly out-of-time feel, as does the chandaliered breakfast room. The hotel's bedrooms feel rather less grand but are very comfortable. They vary in style and size, following the original layout of this rambling mansion house. Light sleepers would be best to ask for a room at the rear of the hotel.

To see and do: the Cathedral and the Giralda, the Jewish Quarter, the Plaza de España and the María Luisa Park

HOSTERÍA DEL LAUREL

MAP: 2

Plaza de los Venerables 5
41004 Sevilla

Tel: 954 220295 or 954 210759 **Fax:** 954 210450

e-mail: host-laurel@hosteriadellaurel.com

Web Page: www.hosteriadellaurel.com

Closed: Never

Bedrooms: 1 Single, 5 Doubles, 21 Twins, 2 Triples and 1 Quadruple

Price: Single €49-67, Double/Twin €70-97, Triple €85-121, Quadruple €103-139 + 7% VAT

Meals: Breakfast included, Lunch/Dinner €30-35 including wine

Getting there: The hotel is at a corner of the Plaza de los Venerables close to the Cathedral. Park in any city-centre car park (the nearest is 'Cano y Cueto' at the junction of Calle Cano y Cueto and Menéndez Pelayo) then take a taxi to the hotel. DON'T TRY TO DRIVE HERE!

Management: David Márquez López

The Plaza de los Venerables is right in the middle of Sevilla's Jewish quarter. Wandering its labyrinth of streets remains a beguiling experience even if you are liable to be occasionally engulfed by a group of camera-toting tourists. At one corner of this pedestrianised square, the Hostería del Laurel has long been one of my favourite Sevilla hotels. It is one of the city's oldest inns and the place supposedly inspired the writer Zorilla when he was penning "*Don Juan*". You enter by way of a rather dark bar-cum-dining room, whose most notable feature is a sea of hams suspended from the ceiling. Added to this are mounted hunting trophies of boar, deer and mountain goats. Beyond is a much lighter, cheery reception area above which are two floors of bedrooms. Choose one on the second floor to get extra insulation from the activity in the restaurant below. The rooms are very well-equipped—TVs, phones, air-conditioning—and most of them are of really generous proportions. The Laurel's prices are more than reasonable given the location. The staff are very helpful, too.

To see and do: the Cathedral and the Giralda, the Jewish Quarter, the Plaza de España and the María Luisa Park

TABERNA DEL ALABARDERO

MAP: 2

Zaragoza 20
41001 Sevilla

Tel: 954 560637 or 954 502721 **Fax:** 954 563666

e-mail: hotel.alabardero@esh.es

Web Page: www.grupolezama.com

Closed: August

Bedrooms: 1 Double, 3 Twins and 3 Suites

Price: Double/Twin €145, Suite €178 + 7% VAT

Meals: Breakfast included, Lunch €10-14 including wine, Dinner €45 (*menu de degustación*) including wine

Getting there: In the city centre take Paseo de Colón passing Torre del Oro. Immediately in front of the Triana bridge turn right and then take the third right to Alabardero. The hotel has its own car park. Staff will park your car for you.

Management: Don Luis Lezama Barañano

This elegant Sevilla mansion house was the home of the poet
Cavestany whose most notable literary creation was *A la Sombra de
la Giralda* ("Under the Giralda's Shadow"). You are, indeed, just a
shake away from Sevilla's most emblematic architectural feature and
very close to the Maestranza bullring. The hotel was born in 1992
after lengthy and meticulous restoration work. Its focus is a graceful
patio courtyard, a popular rendezvous for well-heeled *Sevillanos* who
meet for breakfast, and for tea and cakes in the afternoon. The restaurant is amongst the city's best (it won a Michelin star and was a
favourite of the King's mother) and you dine in one of a series of
exquisitely decorated, wonderfully intimate dining rooms. The
culinary philosophy is *cocina de mercado* (whatever is in season)
with a predilection for game. If you go for the lunchtime menu in the
cafetería it won't cost an arm or a leg. Bedrooms are regal affairs.
They have parquet floors with excellent linen and mattresses and a
host of details such as embroidered bath robes, hydro-massage baths,
air-conditioning and handsome fabrics for bedspreads and curtains.
Well worth a splurge.

To see and do: the Cathedral and the Giralda, the Jewish Quarter,
the Plaza de España and the María Luisa Park

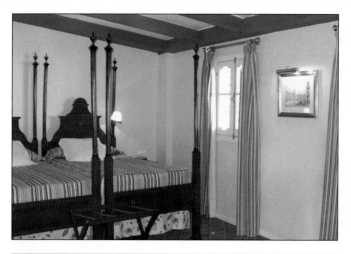

LAS CASAS DE LA JUDERIA

MAP: 2

Callejón Dos Hermanas 7
41004 Sevilla

Tel: 954 415150 **Fax:** 954 422170

e-mail: juderia@casasypalacios.com

Web Page: www.casasypalacios.com

Closed: Never

Bedrooms: 7 Singles, 97 Doubles/Twins/Junior Suites and 3 Suites

Price: Single €97-101, Double/Twin €128-156,
Junior Suite €147-174, Suite €218-250 + 7% VAT

Meals: Breakfast €15, no Lunch or Dinner available. There are
several good restaurants and bars within walking distance.

Getting there: Callejón Dos Hermanas is just off the Calle Esteban,
close to the Murillo gardens in the Santa Cruz quarter. Best to park in
Cano y Cueto car park at the junction of Calle Cano y Cueto and
Menéndez Pelayo and take a taxi to the hotel (or walk the 2 minutes
from here to the hotel).

Management: Miguel Cazorla Cuadro

There are still parts of Sevilla's Santa Cruz where *cafés* and bars outnumber souvenir shops and where you can get a feel for genuine *Sevillano* life. Las Casas de la Judería is just beyond the tourist tract and is reached by way of a quiet *cul-de-sac*. Several townhouses once owned by the Duke of Béjar make up this rich southern fantasy of interconnecting patios, gurgling fountains, ferns, geraniums, orange trees and aspidistra. Every corner of the hotel seems to offer respite from the heat and dust of the city. There are quiet, parquet-floored lounges where old oils, comfy sofas, carefully arranged flowers and stacks of magazines make you feel like they've been lifted from a Kensington mews. Everywhere you look, one of the hotel's staff is polishing, sweeping, carrying a bag or delivering a gin and tonic. Bedrooms are as elegant as you might expect and surprisingly quiet. The "junior" suites are well worth the extra euros. Although larger than most places we include in this book, this hotel remains one of the city's more seductive addresses and has more than a hint of Raffles.

To see and do: the Cathedral and the Giralda, the Jewish Quarter, the Plaza de España and the María Luisa Park

EL TRIGUERO

MAP: 2

Ctra Carmona-El Viso del Alcor km 29
41410 Carmona

Tel: 955 953626 or 636 844242 **Fax:** 955 953626

Closed: Never

Bedrooms: 2 Doubles and 7 Twins

Price: Double/Twin €48, larger Double/Twin 58 + 7% VAT

Meals: Breakfast included, Lunch/Dinner €15 including wine.
Advance warning is necessary.

Getting there: From Carmona take the N-392 towards El Viso del
Alcor (also signposted for *Lidl* supermarket)). At the km 29 marker
post turn left and follow the track to El Triguero.

Management: Carmen Vega Salguero

There are still places to stay in Andalusia where simple comfort takes precedence over satellite TV and jacuzzi bath tubs. If you're happy to sleep far from shops, bars and the rumble of traffic, if you don't mind swapping a gleaming hotel reception for a kindly house-keeper whose English is of the "good...please?" variety, if you're happy with simple country cooking rather than burgers and pizza, then this is your place. The alluring *cortijo* (farm) stands alone on a low ridge looking out across kilometre after kilometre of farmland, the breadbasket of Sevilla. Seeing the sunset here and feeling the silence of night wrap around the house is an experience you'll never forget. El Triguero is far more home than hotel. You'll find family portraits and photographs, etchings and oils, simple yet elegant bed-rooms and whirling fans to keep the heat at bay. Do find time for a walk out through the estate by way of the sandy citrus grove that laps up to El Triguero. Try to book the tower room, forgive the rather uninspired offering at breakfast and rejoice in the place's authenticity.

To see and do: visits to Carmona, Sevilla and Osuna

HOTEL PALACIO MARQUÉS DE LA GOMERA

MAP: 3

Calle San Pedro 20
41640 Osuna

Tel: 954 812223 **Fax:** 954 810200

e-mail: palaciogomera@telefonica.net

Web Page: www.hotelpalaciodelmarques.com

Closed: Never

Bedrooms: 2 Doubles, 18 Twins and 2 Suites

Price: Double €108-120, Twin €84-90, Suite €156-180 + 7% VAT

Meals: Breakfast €10, Lunch/Dinner €28-36 including wine or in patio restaurant in summer approx.€20

Getting there: From Sevilla take the A-92 towards Granada, then take the first exit for Osuna. At the roundabout go straight up Calle Sevilla to Plaza Mayor. Exit at the top left of the square into Calle Carrera. Take the first left after Calle San Pedro, then second left and left again to the hotel.

Management: Francisco José Mulero Molino

One of the great things about living in Andalusia is coming across real gems of towns and villages whose beauty you had never imagined. So it was for me with Osuna, its Calle San Pedro and its remarkable hotel, El Marqués de la Gomera. Nothing quite prepares you for the opulence of its flamboyant portal, its marbled patio and the imposing sweep of its baroque staircase. The building's base element is the golden sandstone that is a characteristic of the town's architecture and which adds warmth and substance to the feel of public rooms and bedrooms. The most remarkable of these is the "Torreón" suite from whose lofty perch you have a wonderful roof-scape view of Osuna. All are special, most are huge, and are decorated with a successful blend of antiques and contemporary colours and furnishings. Bed linen, mattresses and fabrics are all top-of-the-range. You can choose between two restaurants at Gomera—an informal garden restaurant or the Casa del Marqués where, to quote the hotel's young manager Francisco José, the food is 'Andalusian and gourmet'. Whatever your choice, you'll eat extremely well.

To see and do: visits to Osuna, Sevilla and Córdoba

ALGUACILES BAJOS

MAP: 9

Ctra Montellano-Las Cabezas de San Juan km 22.6
Las Cabezas de San Juan

Tel: 630 561529 **Fax:** 91 5641071

e-mail: alguaciles@alguaciles.com

Web Page: www.alguaciles.com

Closed: Never

Bedrooms: 1 Single, 1 Double and 6 Twins

Price: Single €36, Double/Twin €48 + 7 % VAT

Meals: Breakfast included. No other meals are available but 2 simple roadside restaurants are just a short drive from the farm.

Getting there: From Sevilla take the N-IV towards Cádiz to Cabezas de San Juan. Here go left at the crossroads and follow the A-371 towards Villamartín. After approx. 6.5km turn left again on the SE-445 towards Montellano. Alguaciles Bajos is on the left after 3.4km.

Management: Maribel Gómez

If you are tiring of the tourist-beaten track and are keen to get a real feel for life on an Andalusian *cortijo* (farm), book a couple of nights at Alguaciles Bajos. It is lost in the gently rolling hills of the Sevilla *campiña* surrounded by a belt of tall palm trees, miles from the nearest village. Stepping into the farm's 400 year-old cobbled court- yard feels like stepping back into another age. Maribel, the kindly housekeeper, or her son Simon emerge to show you to your room, which will be spacious and decorated with both traditional and mod- ern paintings, a sofa, easy chairs, and a comfortable bed. Add to this a sparkling bathroom, air-conditioning and a fridge. Once you've unpacked and marveled at your room (what incredible value!) be sure to follow a way-marked path out across the estate, through fields of wheat and sunflowers. At sunset this is an exquisite experi- ence. Then drive just a mile or two along the narrowest of country lanes to a fantastic little *venta* where you won't hear anything apart from Spanish being spoken. You'll feel a million miles away from Marbella and, if you're anything like me, thankful that there are still places in Spain which are truly different.

To see and do: Sevilla, Jerez and the white villages of the Grazalema Natural Park

HACIENDA DE SAN RAFAEL

MAP: 9

Apartado de Correos 28
Carretera Nacional IV km 594
41730 Las Cabezas de San Juan

Tel: 955 872193 or 020 85632100 (in the UK)
Fax: 955 872201 or 020 85632300 (in the UK)

e-mail: info@haciendadesanrafael.com

Web Page: www.haciendadesanrafael.com

Closed: 1 November - 31 March

Bedrooms: 7 Doubles, 4 Twins and 3 Cottages

Price: Double/Twin €210, Casita €480 + 7% VAT

Meals: Breakfast included, Lunch €25, Dinner €55 including wine

Getting there: Leave Sevilla following the signs for Cádiz and just before you reach the motorway, branch onto the N-IV. Shortly before Las Cabezas de San Juan, just past the km 594 marker post (be sure to keep well to right and indicate!) turn right and follow the long drive to San Rafael.

Management: Kuky & Tim Reid

The rolling farmlands stretching south from Sevilla have a unique beauty—a vast, open landscape peppered with whitewashed farmsteads over which high, swaying palms stand sentinel. San Rafael is every inch the classic Andalusian *cortijo* (farm). Surrounded by olive groves, its ochre and white frontage gives onto an inner courtyard that is awash with brilliant damask bougainvillaea. Thanks to the decorative razzmatazz and *savoir-faire* of Tim and Kuky Reid, it is has been transformed into one of Andalusia's most exceptional small hotels. Choose between a *casita* (three share their own pool) or one of the mezzanine rooms which have masses of space, walk-in bathrooms and their own verandas. They have been decorated with antiques, contemporary furnishings and pieces collected by the Reids on many travels to the Far East. Relax with a pre-dinner *fino* (dry sherry) in the most comfortable of lounges (olive oil was once stored here) and choose between eating a sumptuous dinner in the dining room or in the privacy of your terrace. A place to go on any special occasion, and what you will celebrate most is having chosen San Rafael.

To see and do: visits to the Sherry bodegas in Jerez, the city of Sevilla, and the Doñana Park

CÁDIZ
PROVINCE

HOTELS 023 TO 046

El Bosque

LOS HELECHOS

MAP: 9

Plaza de Madre de Dios 9
11540 Sanlúcar de Barrameda

Tel: 956 361349 or 956 367655 **Fax:** 956 369650

e-mail: info@hotelloshelechos.com

Web Page: www.hotelloshelechos.com

Closed: Never

Bedrooms: 8 Doubles and 46 Twins

Price: Double/Twin €40-56 + 7% VAT

Meals: Breakfast €4, no Lunch or Dinner available. Several good fish bars and restaurants are within walking distance.

Getting there: From Jerez take the A-480 to Sanlúcar. Here take Avenida del Vº Centenario following the signs 'Centro Ciudad'. Los Helechos is in the lower part of the old town in Calle Baños. If you get lost, just ask for Plazaleta de La Salle.

Management: Manuel Reina de los Reyes

Los Helechos, another Sanlúcar hotel which oozes Andalusia from its every corner, is the fruit of a complete renovation of a turn-of-the century mansion. You enter via a massive oak door which leads through to a marble-flagged patio with geometric tiles, wrought-iron grilles, whitewashed walls and masses of potted ferns (from which the hotel takes its name). To one side is the reception where you are greeted by the friendliest of staff and a statue of the Rocío Virgin. Bedrooms are reached via a series of patios where lemon trees, potted aspidistra and gurgling fountains strike the same southern note. Most look inwards to the patios. Those giving onto the street have double-glazed windows to minimise traffic noise. The rooms are medium-sized, simply furnished, sparkling clean and the nicest of them retain their original floor tiles. You are just a short stroll from the town's delightful palm-fringed square, the Plaza del Cabildo. No visit to the town is complete without a pre-dinner *manzanilla* and a *tapa* of *tortilla de camarones* (shrimps deep-fried in batter) at Casa Balbino.

To see and do: visits to the Doñana Park, the *salinas* (salt beds), the pine forest of Monte Algaida, the old town of Sanlúcar and the *manzanilla bodegas*

POSADA DE PALACIO

MAP: 9

Calle Caballeros 11
11540 Sanlúcar de Barrameda

Tel: 956 364840 **Fax:** 956 365060

e-mail: posadadepalacio@terra.es

Web Page: www.posadadepalacio.com

Closed: Mid January - mid February

Bedrooms: 4 Doubles, 6 Twins and 4 Suites

Price: Double/Twin with shower €65-75,
Double/Twin with bath €75 -90, Suite €95-120 + 7% VAT

Meals: Breakfast €6

Getting there: As you arrive in Sanlúcar on the A-480 bear right at
the petrol station. At the roundabout continue straight on and at the
next fork, go left into Avenida Doctor Fleming. Pass Barbadillo
Bodega and Parroquía de la O. Posada is on the left.

Management: Carmen Diaz

Most visitors to Sanlúcar de Barrameda come to see the enormous bodegas where its dry *manzanilla* wine is produced. There are a host of other reasons for coming—to make a boat trip up the River Guadalquivir, to visit Doñana, to wander its lively covered markets, to eat fish fresh off the slab, to visit a place which remains unscathed by mass tourism and to stay at the delightful Posada de Palacio. This rambling mansion seems to encapsulate the mood of the town—sleepy and beguiling, with an air of past glories. An inner patio sets the mood, with ferns, a well, old flags and the classical *albero* ochre picking out detail on elegant mouldings. The Posada's rooms vary, following the twists and turns of the building. While some are vast, others are smaller, some have sitting rooms or balconies, but all are unaffectedly charming. I always look forward to breakfast here; great coffee, freshly squeezed orange juice and the thought of a day in this wonderful town. The Posada's owners have recently thoroughly revamped and redecorated the place.

To see and do: visits to the Doñana Park, the *salinas* (salt beds) and pine forest of Monte Algaida, *manzanilla bodegas* and the old town of Sanlúcar

HOSTAL BAHÍA

MAP: 9

Plocia 5
11005 Cádiz

Tel: 956 259110 or 956 259061 **Fax:** 956 254208

e-mail: hostalbahia@terra.es

Web Page: www.infocadiz.com

Closed: Never

Bedrooms: 6 Doubles and 15 Twins

Price: Double/Twin €45 including VAT

Meals: No meals available, but several bars and restaurants within walking distance

Getting there: Arriving in Cádiz follow the signs for *casco antiguo*. Park in the underground car park of Plaza del Ayuntamiento. Calle Plocia is just off the east side of the Plaza.

Management: Ramón García

Unless you're feeling flush enough to stay at the Atlántico (too large for this guide), finding a decent place to stay in the old town of Cádiz isn't easy. When researching this guide, I visited a dozen places on the trail of that "perfect small Cádiz hotel," but it just isn't there. However, Hostal Bahía is a good compromise if simple, no-frills comfort is enough for you. This unassuming hostal is just off the Plaza de San Juan Dios, the centre of the old town. It's easy to spot its salmon-coloured façade. The staff are friendly, and their English is basic. Downstairs is a tiny reception area, beyond which a marble staircase leads to three floors of bedrooms. These are smallish, but pleasant, with pine furniture and fitted wardrobes. Air-conditioning and satellite TV are unexpected bonuses given the price of the rooms. No breakfast is served but you are just metres from the terrace *cafés* of the Plaza, a lovely place to start the day with *tostadas* and coffee. Or it's only a five minute walk to the Plaza de Abastos for *chocolate con churros* (hot chocolate with Andalusian-style donuts)!

To see and do: visits to the old city of Cádiz, the quayside, fortifications and the Alameda gardens, boat trip across the bay to El Puerto de Santa María

HOTEL LOS OLIVOS DEL CONVENTO

MAP: 9

Paseo de Boliches 30
11630 Arcos de la Frontera

Tel: 956 700811 **Fax:** 956 702018

e-mail: losolivosdelc@terra.es

Web Page: http://losolivos.profesionales.org

Closed: Never

Bedrooms: 2 Singles, 5 Doubles and 12 Twins

Price: Single €40-45, Double/Twin €60-70 including VAT

Meals: Breakfast €6, no Lunch or Dinner available but good food in the sister restaurant El Convento. Lunch there is approximately €25 including wine, and dinner is approximately €30 excluding wine.

Getting there: Arriving in Arcos follow signs for the Parador. As you follow the one-way system up into the old part of town you'll see the hotel just to the left of the road.

Management: José Antonio Roldán Caro

José Roldán Caro is, as the Spanish would say, *un fenómeno* (phenomenal). Owner of another Arcos hotel and the town's best restaurant, organiser of gastronomic and cultural events promoting his beloved Arcos, he still somehow manages to find time to manage Los Olivos and personally attend to diners at his restaurant—with considerable grace, to boot. Los Olivos, his second hotel, is as Andalusian as the man himself. You pass it as you climb up into the old town centre—a brilliant white, terracotta-tiled façade with arched balcony and beautiful wrought-iron *rejas* (window/door grilles). No surprise that the Andalusian flag (along with the Spanish one) hangs above the door. The hotel's focal point is a plant-filled patio surrounded by a covered gallery with comfortable cane sofas and arm chairs. A wide sweep of staircase leads to the sparkling bedrooms, some looking out to the valley beneath Arcos, others facing the inner patio (light sleepers would prefer one of these). Los Olivos' staff are incredibly friendly and so are its prices.

To see and do: the old town of Arcos, the *bodegas* and Royal Equestrian School in Jerez, the Grazalema Natural Park and the white villages

CORTIJO BARRANCO

MAP: 10

Apartado de Correos 169
11630 Arcos de la Frontera

Tel: 956 231402 **Fax:** 956 231209

e-mail: reservas@cortijobarranco.com

Web Page: www.cortijobarranco.com

Closed: Never

Bedrooms: 10 Doubles, 5 Twins and 5 Apartments

Price: Double/Twin €67, Apartment €90-121 including VAT

Meals: Breakfast €3, Lunch €5-15, Dinner €15-22 including wine, weekdays only

Getting there: From Arcos de la Frontera take the A-372 towards El Bosque. After 5.7km, at the end of a long straight section, turn left at the sign for Barranco then follow a track for 2km to the farm.

Management: María José Gil Amián

Barranco, of all the *cortijo* (farm) hotels of Andalusia, is perhaps the one that gives you the best feeling for how life on one of these vast country estates is lived. Cutting in from the Arcos road, follow three kilometers of track upwards, then round a final bend to the farm which is adrift in a landscape of olives and wheat fields. Massive walls defy the Andalusian sun and crenelated towers remind you that this was once *frontera* (frontier) country. The farm wraps round a classic, arched inner courtyard where you are greeted by the Gil Amián family or Barranco's resident housekeepers before being shown to your room. The leitmotiv here is unaffected, old-fashioned comfort—good linen, antique bedsteads with thick mattresses and, bright *kilims* contrasted against the traditional whitewashed walls. The comfortable lounge has a billiards table and honesty bar. Served in a beautiful high-ceilinged dining room, Barranco's breakfasts and candlelit dinners are excellent. Quiet, remote and enchanting. Even horse rides can be organised through Barranco's estate.

To see and do: Arcos de la Frontera and Medina Sidonia, the Grazalema Natural Park, the *bodegas* and Royal Equestrian School in Jerez

LA CASA GRANDE

MAP: 9

Calle Maldonado 10
11630 Arcos de la Frontera

Tel: 956 703930 **Fax:** 956 717095

e-mail: info@lacasagrande.net

Web Page: www.lacasagrande.net

Closed: 15 December - 27 December

Bedrooms: 3 Doubles, 1 Twin and 2 Suites

Price: Double/Twin €70, Suite €82-88 + 7% VAT

Meals: Breakfast €6.5, tapas-style lunches and suppers €18-25 including wine

Getting there: Follow the signs up to the Parador. It's narrow but unless you have a wide vehicle it can be done! Park in the square in front of the Parador. Walk to the end of Calle Escribano (narrow street to the left of the Parador), turn right, pass Hotel El Convento and then turn left. La Casa Grande is on the right.

Management: Elena Posa

There is, of course, an art to good living, and the Spanish are perhaps the Europeans who live the Epicurean ideal to the fullest. A stay at La Casa Grande as guest of this immensely intelligent, attractive Catalan couple is certainly one of the better things in life. Its location is incredible. This 276 year-old house nudges right up to the very edge of the Arcos cliff. It is a classic *seigneurial* townhouse with a grand portal, columned inner patio and huge reception rooms, three floors high. Elena and Ferrán have given the house new life by creating four guest bedrooms and suites in its upper floors and decorating them with considerable panache, happily mixing the original traditional Andalusian features (there are wonderful original floors) with contemporary colours and Ikea-ish furnishings. La Casa Grande's breakfast is a feast of orange juice, cheese, wonderful bread and a *degustación* (a tasting) of different olive oils. But what you will most remember is its rooftop terrace where Elena will serve you a light, *tapas* supper. The views from here are simply beyond belief.

To see and do: the old town of Arcos, the *bodegas* and Royal Equestrian School in Jerez, the white villages, and the villages of the Sierra de Grazalema

HOTEL REAL DE VEAS

MAP: 9

Corredera 12
11630 Arcos de la Frontera

Tel: 956 717370 **Fax:** 956 717369

e-mail: hotelrealdeveas@hotmail.com

Closed: Never

Bedrooms: 6 Doubles, 4 Twins and 2 Suites

Price: Standard Double/Twin €68-72, Superior Double/Twin €79-82, Suite €95-100 + 7% VAT

Meals: Breakfast €4.50 (but included in low season), Dinners also occasionally available for approx. €15

Getting there: Arriving in Arcos follow signs for the Parador de Turismo. After passing Hotel Los Olivos del Convento take the next left into Calle Julio Mariscal. Go to the end of this street and you'll see Hotel Real de Veas immediately opposite.

Management: Mari Angeles & Cristobal Santana

There are almost a dozen great places to stay in and around Arcos de la Frontera. Hotel Real de Veas, high on my personal list of favourites, is a grand 19th century townhouse that has recently been thoroughly refurbished by its charming owners, Mari-Angeles and Cristobal Santana. The hotel is just metres from the Cathedral and on one of the town's liveliest thoroughfares. Stepping in from the street you'll be greeted with a smile then shown to a central patio where light streams in through the magnificent original atrium. Bedrooms all lead off this inner *sanctum* and have been decorated in pastel colours with attractive carved 'Ronda-style' furniture. They have all the extras that you'd expect in a much larger hotel—televisions, mini bars, safe boxes, air-conditioning and even hydromassage baths—and they all shine like the newest pin. Breakfast is normally the only meal on offer but given sufficient warning, Mari-Angeles can also prepare supper. She makes a wonderful *paella* and the accompanying house wine is excellent. Or you may choose instead to head off and rub shoulders with the locals in one of Arcos' many *tapas* bars.

To see and do: the old town of Arcos, the white villages and the 'route of the lakes'

HACIENDA BUENA SUERTE

MAP: 10

Apartado de Correos 60
11650 Villamartín

Tel: 956 231286 **Fax:** 956 231275

e-mail: magda-dysli@gmx.de

Web Page: www.dysli.net

Closed: Never

Bedrooms: 2 Singles, 4 Doubles, 5 Twins, 1 Triple and 1 Apartment.

Price: Single €42, Double/Twin €74, Triple €98,
Apartment €980 weekly

Meals: Breakfast included, Lunch €15, Dinner €18 including wine

Getting there: From Ronda take the A-376 towards Sevilla, then the A-382 towards Jerez. 7km before Villamartín turn left for El Bosque/Ubrique. The large white entrance gate to the Hacienda is on the left, 1.5km after you turn off the A-382.

Management: Magda & Jean-Claude Dysli

In the last foothills of the Grazalema mountains, surrounded by a vast estate of olive groves and indigenous oak forest, Hacienda Buena Suerte is a great choice for anyone with an interest in horses. Jean-Claude Dysli gives lessons in Western-style riding. He is one of the world's best instructors, dividing his time between the USA, Spain and his native Switzerland. You won't see finer quarter horses in Europe and even as an equine ignoramus I found it fascinating to watch his pupils being put through their paces. The stables are just across from the main *cortijo* (farm) which is graced by high palm trees and rampant bougainvillaea. In the bedrooms the emphasis is on uncluttered comfort with prints of horses and animal skins giving them a rather Wild West, frontier-country feel. Life at Buena Suerte centres round a huge beamed dining-room/bar where lunches and dinners are eaten at big bench tables. Much of what you eat is farm-raised and organically grown. You don't have to be a rider to enjoy the beautiful walks thoughout the estate.

To see and do: riding with Jean-Claude and Magda, visits to the Grazalema Natural Park, Ronda, Sevilla and Jerez

LA CARMELA

MAP: 9

Carril El Atravesado
El Palmar
11150 Vejer de la Frontera

Tel: 609 405966 or 956 232909 **Fax:** 956 232909

Web Page: www.lacarmela.com

Closed: October-Easter

Bedrooms: 3 Doubles and 4 Twins

Price: Double/Twin €50-70 including VAT and breakfast

Meals: Breakfast included

Getting there: From the N-340, exit at km23 towards Conil. At the first roundabout turn left towards Caños de Meca and after 7kms (at the next roundabout) go right. Follow the road to the sea then turn left and at end of this road go left, heading inland. Take the next left and La Carmela is on the left.

Management: Isabel Iglesias & Ignacio Elosegui

If you are looking for a great place to stay near some of the Atlantic coast's best beaches, look no further than this small, modern guest house. Isabel and Ignacio, two young, cosmopolitan Spaniards from the Basque country, have transformed what was once a run-of-the-mill beachside villa into an oasis of colour and tranquility. The original building was extended to create an inner courtyard which has been planted with ficus, jasmine, lavender and bougainvilleas. Seven of the eight bedrooms give on to this feast of greenery. They have Casablanca fans, interesting prints of modern art and antique cupboards and dressers. The overall feel is clean, uncluttered and restful. There is a massive lounge (with an enormous collection of music) which leads out to a terrace where breakfasts are served. Just beyond, the pool is surrounded by a big sweep of garden with loungers tucked into its shadiest corners. Isabel and Ignacio are mindful of your privacy yet attentive, especially if you need their help planning excursions or choosing a good place to eat.

To see and do: the beach of El Palmar, Vejer and the white villages, golf and riding at Montenmedio

CASACINCO

MAP: 9

Calle Sancho IV El Bravo 5
11150 Vejer de la Frontera

Tel: 956 455029 or 626 481301 **Fax:** 956 451125

e-mail: info@hotelcasacinco.com

Web Page: www.hotelcasacinco.com

Closed: January

Bedrooms: 3 Doubles and 1 Twin

Price: Double/Twin €70-90 including breakfast.
Minimum stay is 2 nights.

Meals: Breakfast included, no meals but masses of restaurants within walking distance

Getting there: From Algeciras take the N-340 north-west towards Cádiz then take the second turning left for Vejer at km 36. Go up the hill and when you reach town follow the signs for *Ayuntamiento*. When you reach the Plaza de España park car, go through the arch at the top of square and take the first right. CasaCinco is on your left.

Management: Colette Bardell-Murphy & Glen Murphy

Vejer de la Frontera has the unusual credentials of being both a hill-top and coastal town, a sort of Ronda by-the-sea. It's puzzling that it has only recently attracted the attention of northern Europeans in search of their Shangri-La. At the heart of the old town, CasaCinco is one of the most original and intimate places to stay on the Atlantic coast. Appealing to all five sense, taste is the one that you'll remember most. Breakfasts here are inspired and they vary with Colette's mood and the season. We were treated to a fabulous fruit kebab wrapped in a crepe with delicious bread and pot-fulls of tea and coffee. Further sensual pleasure came in the sounds of great *flamenco*. Glen can offer good advice should you want to buy a few CDs or search out a *peña* or two. Music is always present at CasaCinco and bedrooms have CDs rather than TVs. Their decoration is inspired, too, eclectically mixing ethnic and modern with semi-open plan bathrooms. It all works really well. Glen and Colette are young, friendly and really do want to make you feel *en tu casa* (at home).

To see and do: whale watching, visits to Jerez *bodegas* and the Royal Equestrian School, good *flamenco* clubs in Barbate and Vejer

LA CASA DEL CALIFA

MAP: 9

Plaza de España 16
11150 Vejer de la Frontera

Tel: 956 447730 **Fax:** 956 451625

e-mail: hotel@vejer.com

Web Page: www.vejer.com/califa

Closed: Never

Bedrooms: 1 Single, 7 Doubles, 7 Twins and 2 Suites

Price: Single €42-49, Double/Twin €55-72, Special Double/Twin
€78-92, Suite €92-105 + 7% VAT

Meals: Breakfast included, Lunch/Dinner approximately
€30 including wine

Getting there: From Algeciras take the N-340 north-west towards
Cádiz. Then take the second turning left for Vejer at km 36. Go up
the hill and when you reach town follow the signs for *Ayuntamiento*.
When you reach the Plaza de España, the Casa del Califa is on
your left.

Management: Regli Alvárez & James Stuart

The history of Andalusia is wrapped in the fabric of La Casa de la Califa's ancient walls. An ancient road—Roman or perhaps even Phoenician—girdles its garden, the Moors chose the spot to build a huge *aljibe* (water tank) and the Christians added an enormous grain store. It is said that the Inquisition officiated here and later the Nationalists used the place as a barracks in the Civil War. In the most recent chapter of the place's fascinating history the five houses that make up the present building have been converted into a gorgeous small hotel whose fascinating labyrinth of twists, turns, staircases and patios is the very antithesis of the 'off-the-peg' chain hotel. Bedrooms are all different in size and configuration, many grab views of Vejer's wonderful roof line. The rooms are stylish, comfortable and uncluttered. In a patio-garden which has been sculpted into rock at the rear of the building you dine beneath citrus trees, enjoying the North African-inspired cuisine. Like Vejer itself, this small hotel will soon seduce you with its charm.

To see and do: the Natural Park of Los Alcornocales, great beaches like that of El Palmar, visits to the *bodegas* in Jerez

CORTIJO DE LA PLATA

MAP: 9

Ctra Atlanterra km 4
11393 Zahara de los Atunes

Tel: 956 439001 **Fax:** 956 439456

e-mail: hotel@cortijodelaplata.com

Web Page: www.cortijodelaplata.com

Closed: Early December - middle March

Bedrooms: 1 Single, 6 Doubles, 7 Twins and 1 Apartment

Price: Double/Twin with bath €66-96, Double/Twin with shower €60-83 + 7% VAT

Meals: Breakfast €6, Lunch/Dinner approx.€30 including wine

Getting there: Arriving in Zahara de los Atunes follow signs for the Melía Atlántico for 3km to Urbanización Atlanterra. The hotel is signposted here, just to the left of the road.

Management: José María Castrillón Quintela

Cortijo de la Plata may ring a bell in some ears. This was one of the very first hotels on the Costa de la Plata, the home of one Lord Brudenell Bruce who converted the stables of an old army barracks into a small hotel where he could lodge his many friends. Later, groups of ornithologists came for the spectacle of annual migrations to and from Africa. More recently (the place lay empty after Lord Bruce's death) Chelo and José María Castrillón have given the building a new lease on life with their flair for decoration and determination to make every corner of the place truly special. Furnishings, fittings and fabrics were chosen with authenticity and comfort in mind. In the courtyards and gardens hibiscus, vines, palms and cacti were planted as well as lawns and an organic vegetable patch. The views down to the beach, excellent fish and vegetables served in the intimate restaurant, the decorative charm of the bedrooms and the friendliness of its hosts help make this one of Andalusia's most special small hotels.

To see and do: Vejer de la Frontera, the roman ruins of Baelo Claudio, the cliffs of the La Breña pine forest

LA HORMIGA VOLADORA

MAP: 9

El Lentiscal 18
Bolonia Tarifa

Tel: 956 688562 **Fax:** 956 688562

Closed: Never

Bedrooms: 7 Doubles, 4 Twins and 3 Apartments

Price: Double/Twin €48-60, Apartment €66-78 including VAT

Meals: Breakfasts (only served from 15 July - 15 September) approximately €5

Getting there: From Algeciras head north on the N-340 towards Cádiz. Pass Tarifa and at km 70 turn left at signs for Bolonia. As you arrive in the village, turn left at the Bella Vista Hostal. The road soon bears hard to the left and after 100m you'll see the Hormiga Voladora on the right.

Management: Julia Muñoz Fernández & Rafael Chico Jimenez

If you ask most folk who know Andalusia's Atlantic coast which is their favourite beach you can be fairly certain what the answer will be. Bolonia. Not only does it have a beautiful arc of sand and dunes and some great fish restaurants but also, just yards from the beach, are the Roman ruins of Baelo Claudio. The garum paste that was made here sometimes ended on the very best tables in Rome. There are a couple of bog-standard *hostals* in the village and masses of dull apartments but by far the nicest place to stay is La Hormiga Voladora. This simple little hostelry is right next to the sea, surrounded by a thick stand of bamboo. If you've ever been here with the *levante* wind blowing you'll understand why it hasn't been cut down to open up views of the sea. The hostal's bedrooms are simple, almost Spartan, but perfectly adequate. Some have bathrooms en suite and others have shower rooms reached by crossing a small courtyard. Breakfasts, in season, are served in a pretty patio beneath a huge mulberry tree and Rafael and Julia, the friendly owners, can recommend where to eat the best fish in the village.

To see and do: whale and dolphin-watching excursions, the Roman ruins of Baelo Claudio and day trips to Morocco

100% FUN

MAP: 10

Ctra Cádiz Km 76
11380 Tarifa

Tel: 956 680330 or 956 680013 **Fax:** 956 680013

e-mail: 100x100@tnet.es

Web Page: www.tarifanet/100fun.es

Closed: 1 November - 28 February

Bedrooms: 8 standard Twins, 8 superior Twins and 6 Quadruples

Price: Single €65-85, Standard Twin €75-92,
Superior Twin €85-102, Quadruple €120-140 including VAT

Meals: Breakfast €6, Lunch/Dinner €15 including wine. The
restaurant is open from early March - end October.

Getting there: From Cádiz take the N-340 towards Algeciras. When
you reach the Tarifa Beach 100% Fun is on the left next to La
Enseñada, close to the km 76 marker post.

Management: Ula Walters & Barry Pussell

Any wind surfer knows that the beaches of the Costa de la Luz get the best waves in Europe and it's no accident that the world championships are held here. Even if you don't surf, the long sweep of the Tarifa beach couldn't fail to move you, with the mountains of the Rif rising a hazy purple above the thumping Atlantic breakers. The road to Cádiz runs between the 100% Fun and the beach but don't let this put you off staying here. Barry and Ula have sculpted the hotel and gardens so that you forget the tarmac and are instead seduced by the pool, exotic vegetation and the friendly, laid-back feel of the place. The bedrooms and enormous suites are fresh, light and uncluttered, all with whirling Casablanca-style fans. The tropical-style restaurant (you'll feel more comfortable in shorts and sandals than a suit and tie) looks like its just been lifted from a *Bacardi* ad. The menu offers welcome respite from steak and chips—good veggie dishes, some spicy *Tex-Mex* offerings and a few eastern notes as well. The place really does live up to its name.

To see and do: Tarifa and the castle of Guzman 'El Bueno', trips to Gibraltar and Morocco, white villages of Vejer and Castellar

HOTEL PUNTA SUR

MAP: 10

Carretera Cádiz-Málaga km 77
11380 Tarifa

Tel: 956 684326 **Fax:** 956 680472

e-mail: hotelpuntasur@cherrytel.com

Web Page: www.hotelpuntasur.com

Closed: Occasionally in winter - check!

Bedrooms: 16 Doubles, 6 Twins, 6 Triples and 4 family Bungalows

Price: Double €71-125, Triple €96-134, Bungalows sleeping 4-5
€120-212+ 7% VAT

Meals: Breakfast included, Lunch €21, Dinner €27 including wine

Getting there: From Cádiz take the N-340 south towards Algeciras.
Hotel Punta Sur is to the left of the N-340 close to km post 77.

Management: Juan Antonio Nuñez

James Whaley is a master in the art of transforming hotels and hostals which may have seem doomed to remain commonplace into some of the most innovative, stylish and spicy places to stay on the Atlantic coast. He had a fantastic site and gardens when he turned his hand to Punta Sur but a year on the bungalow-style rooms have seen complete metamorphosis. He didn't limit himself to the nearest Ikea when it came to decorating Punta Sur; instead he headed for North Africa, the USA, even Indonesia, in search of floors, prints, lamps and photographs. Each bedroom has been decorated to evoke a different place in the world like Bali, Java, Cuba, Congo, Miami but the decoration never gets out of hand and manages to say a lot with a little. All rooms have private terraces looking across the sweep of lawn that runs up to a massive swimming pool where a friendly crocodile has been given the job of life guard. The restaurant is decorated with huge black and white photographs of Africa and India. The food, too, mixes the best of things local with dishes from further afield. *Note: due to landscaping of gardens, hotel will be closed until Easter 2004.*

To see and do: Roman ruins of Baelo Claudio, Natural Parks of Estrecho de Gibraltar and Los Alcornocales and, of course, kite and wind surfing along the Tarifa coast

HOTEL HURRICANE

MAP: 10

Ctra de Málaga a Cádiz km 78
11380 Tarifa

Tel: 956 684919 **Fax:** 956 680329

e-mail: info@hurricanehotel.com

Web Page: www.hurricanehotel.com

Closed: Never

Bedrooms: 35 Doubles, Twins and Suites

Price: Sea-facing Double/Twin €114, Mountain facing Double/Twin €93, Family Suite €161, Luxury Suite €203 + 7% VAT. Prices will increase approx. 5% in 2004.

Meals: Breakfast €9, Lunch €15, Dinner €30 including wine

Getting there: From Cádiz take the N-340 south. The Hurricane Hotel is to the right of the N-340, approximately 7km before you reach Tarifa. It's signposted.

Management: James Whaley

There's nowhere quite like the Hurricane. The hotel owes its existence to James Whaley who saw in a simple roadside "hostal" a vision of better things to come. In the early years most guests were from the windsurfing community but nowadays people come from all over the globe for the pleasure of staying just metres from the mighty breakers of the Atlantic. They also come for the unique feel of the Hurricane which is laid-back, spicy and different. Add to this the fabulous gardens, two pools, a gym, stables, a wind and kite-surfing school and a terrace looking straight out across the waves to the Rif and you begin to get the measure of the place. The best rooms, naturally, are those with sea views but all are stylish in an understated way with a sculptural/decorative debt to things Moroccan (James used to own the Villa Maroc in Essaouira). The Hurricane's food is a great mix of Spanish and International, the lunchtime buffet is excellent, vegetarians get a great choice of dishes, and, as you might hope, there is plenty of fresh fish on the menu. Always book as early as you can. This is one of the most spicey hotels on the Costa de la Luz.

To see and do: Roman ruins of Baelo Claudio, Natural Parks of Estrecho de Gibraltar and Los Alcornocales

HOTEL LA PEÑA

MAP: 10

Ctra N-340 km 78.4
11380 Tarifa

Tel: 956 681070 **Fax:** 956 681070

Closed: November - Easter

Bedrooms: 4 Doubles and 14 Twins

Price: Double/Twin €66-95 + 7% VAT

Meals: Breakfast included, no Lunch/Dinner available. There is good food at the Hurricane, just across the road.

Getting there: From Tarifa take the N-340 towards Cádiz. Hotel La Peña is at km 78.4, to the right of the N-340 shortly before you reach the Hurricane.

Management: Antonio del Castillo

If you are headed for the Tarifa beaches and can bear to stay just back from the sea, then this friendly small hotel is a brilliant venue. You cut up and away from the busy N-340 along an oleander-lined drive to a low, cherry-coloured building. Its well-tended lawns, the surrounding greenery and its single storey is rather reminiscent of the bungalow-style hotels of India. The Castrillo family take great care of La Peña. The day I visited, paint was being retouched, lawns mown and floors polished, yet they still gave me plenty of their time. Their bedrooms either give on to a quiet patio to the rear of the bar/reception (numbers 10-18) or are in an annex just back from the pool (numbers 1-9), from where there are views of Morocco. Most of them are large, spotless, have firm mattresses, large fitted wardrobes and are painted in a fresh, lemony colour (so don't mind those sugary prints). Although only breakfast and drinks are served in the small, plant-filled restaurant-cum-reception, you can walk to the Hurricane for dinner or head into Tarifa for good eats.

To see and do: Tarifa beaches, windsurfing, whale-watching, Roman ruins of Baelo Claudio at Bolonia, day trip to Morocco by ferry or hydrofoil

POSADA LA SACRISTÍA

MAP: 10

San Donato 8
11380 Tarifa

Tel: 956 681759 **Fax:** 956 685182

e-mail: tarifa@lasacristia.net

Web Page: www.lasacristia.net

Closed: Never

Bedrooms: 6 Doubles and 4 Twins

Price: Double/Twin €98-115 including breakfast

Meals: Breakfast included, Dinners (only available at weekends in winter) €20 excluding wine

Getting there: From Algeciras take the N-340 towards Cádiz then take the first exit for Tarifa. Follow the signs to the port and leave your car at a car park just inside of the port gates. From here it is just a two minute walk to the hotel.

Management: Miguel Arregui & Bosco Herrero

'Fusion' is the buzz word in Tarifa at the moment, a pick-and-mixing of the best of European, Eastern and African culture with an occasional dash of California for good measure. You feel it in the music of the Atlantic coast, in its surf-meets-Spain culture and in the vogue for rediscovering its flavours of arab-andalusian cuisine. La Sacristía celebrates this trend and was the brainchild of two Spanish designers and a New York interior decorator. In creating a hotel and restaurant they have also recuperated an old tradition: 300 years ago there was a popular *cantina* right here. The first surprise comes in the patio reception which doubles as a bar (beer pump next to the bookings sheet!) and a shop that sells jewelry, wraps from Thailand and the sort of clothes that you'd feel good in after a day of kite or wind surfing. Bedrooms, too, stylishly mix antiques from the West with lamps and prints from the East. In the adjacent restaurant breakfast is of continental variety whilst dinners go international. Or there are masses of tapas bars and restaurants just yards away in Tarifa's buzzy old-town centre.

To see and do: the old town of Tarifa, whale watching and day trips to Morocco

HOSTAL ATRIUM SAN ROQUE

MAP: 10

Coronel Moscoso 3
11360 San Roque

Tel: 956 780266 **Fax:** 956 780266

e-mail: info@atriumsanroque.com

Web Page: www.atriumsanroque.com

Closed: February

Bedrooms: 2 Singles, 3 Doubles, 7 Twins, and 2 Suites

Price: Single €20, Twin/Double €35-45,
Suite sleeping up to 4 €90 including VAT

Meals: Breakfast €4.50

Getting there: From the N-340, take Exit 119 (at the sign for San Roque). At the first roundabout, take the second exit into the Posada de la Torre, then take the first left and park. Coronel Moscoso is the first street on the right and the *hostal* is on the right, after 100m.

Management: Sandar & Peter Lauffer

Although it is very close to the Costa del Sol, Sotogrande and Gibraltar, the town of San Roque has an easy, utterly *andaluz* and slightly out-of-time feel to it. So too this charming small hotel which lies at the heart of the old town which was recently been given national-monument status. The place feels like the set of a Graham Greene novel—open central courtyard with palms and a fountain and a bannistered marble staircase leading up to the bedrooms. Many of these maintain their original 19th century features—windows with panes of coloured glass, beautiful old floor tiles, painted ceilings and stucco mouldings. Most rooms have their own bathrooms and they vary in size and configuration following the original floor plan of the house. This would be a great place to return after a day spent fishing, bird-watching or riding. The owners are friendly, Rambo the cat equally so, and there are masses of good bars and restaurants when it comes to heading out for dinner. The hotel takes its name, as you might guess, from a magnificent atrium which brings light streaming into the hotel's cheery central patio. Great value, too.

To see and do: visit Gibraltar, whale and dolphin watching trips and fast ferries to Morocco

CASA CONVENTO LA ALMORAIMA

MAP: 10

Ctra Algeciras-Ronda
11350 Castellar de la Frontera

Tel: 956 693002 **Fax:** 956 693214

Web Page: www.la-almoraima.com

Closed: Never

Bedrooms: 3 Singles, 1 Double and 13 Twins

Price: Single €55, Twin €69, Double €90 including VAT

Meals: Breakfast €6, Lunch/Dinner €20 including wine

Getting there: From Algeciras take the N-340 towards Málaga then branch onto the C-331 towards Jimena de la Frontera. La Almoraima is signposted to the left close to the turning for Castellar de la Frontera.

Management: Lidia Espinosa

Almoraima has a colourful history. It was built as a convent by the Countess of Castellar in 1603 and later snatched by the Duke of Medinacelli and became a hunting lodge. Sacked by Napoleon's troops, it was then expropriated by the state and given back to the Medinacelli family only to be sold to a bank, which went bust. Finally it was once again expropriated and turned into one of Andalusia's most seductive hotels. Although Almoraima's balustraded façade and Florentine belfry are a rather grand *entrée*, once you enter its cloistered patio you are enveloped in a magical and intimate world-within-a-world, where plants, birdsong and the scent of orange blossoms are conducive to blissful relaxation. The bedrooms are sober and comfortable, there's an elegant lounge with an honesty bar and authentic Andalusian cuisine which is simple rather than gourmet, served in a chandaliered dining room. Should you stay here you won't want for space—you are surrounded by 16,000 hectares of estate which is yours to explore on foot or on horseback. Be sure to visit nearby Castellar de la Frontera.

To see and do: visits to Castellar de la Fontera and the Natural Park of Los Alcornocales, day trips to Gibraltar and Morocco

HOSTAL EL ANÓN

MAP: 10

Calle Consuelo 34-40
11330 Jimena de la Frontera

Tel: 956 640416 or 956 640113 **Fax:** 956 641110

e-mail: elanon@viautil.com

Web Page: www.andalucia.com

Closed: 2 weeks end June and 2 weeks end November

Bedrooms: 2 Singles, 5 Twins 2 Triples, 2 Quadruple and 1 Apartment

Price: Single €33, Double/Twin €56, Triple €80, Quadruple €100, Apartment €64 including VAT

Meals: Breakfast included, Lunch/Dinner approximately €25 including wine. Bar snacks are also available. The restaurant and bar are closed on Wednesdays.

Getting there: From Málaga take the motorway west towards Algeciras. Exit for Castellar. Go through Valderrama. Cross the railway bridge, then turn right on the A-369 to Jimena. El Anon is in the village centre, signposted to the left.

Management: Suzanna Odell

Susie Odell has lived in Jimena for many years and opened El Anon long before the hilltop villages of this part of Spain became known by the ex-pat community. A number of village houses were gradually wrapped into the fabric of the *hostal* (a simple inn), creating an intimate, organic and delightfully rambling place to stay. Each bedroom is different to the next. Some give onto inner patio-courtyards, others to the village's whitewashed streets, making some of them light, others less so. The emphasis is on simple, rustic, uncluttered comfort rather than on gadgetry and four-star finery. You can see why El Anon's rooms appeal to walkers and the place is popular with groups from the UK who use it as a base from which to explore the paths through the Alcornocales Natural Park. The restaurant and bar feel as cosy as the rest of the hotel. Breakfasts include home-made bread and fresh orange juice and the lunch and dinner menu looks to Spain and Morocco for its inspiration. The staff are young and friendly and the whole place is imbued by Susie's relaxed and friendly nature.

To see and do: Jimena's castle, walks along the Hozgarganta river valley and the cave paintings of Laja Alta

POSADA LA CASA GRANDE

MAP: 10

Calle Fuentenueva 42
11330 Jimena de la Frontera

Tel: 956 640578 **Fax:** 956 640491

e-mail: tcag@eresmas.net

Web Page: www.posadalacasagrande.com

Closed: Never

Bedrooms: 3 Doubles and 2 Twins sharing 3 baths and WCs and
2 Apartments with en suite bathrooms

Price: Double/Twin €35-40, Apartment €75 including VAT

Meals: Breakfast €4, no Lunch/Dinner available, but great *tapas* in
the bar next door

Getting there: From Málaga take the N-340 west towards Cádiz. At
the roundabout in Pueblo Nuevo de Guadiaro turn right to San
Martín del Tesorillo. Here take he CA-513 west and then turn right
onto the A-369 to Jimena. Follow the main street through the village
and take the last right down the hill to La Casa Grande.

Management: Tom & Anna Andrésen

Tom Andrésen isn't the sort of guy who sits around twiddling his thumbs. Since retiring from a life on the North Sea rigs and establishing his home in Jimena he not only restores and sells village houses but, together with his wife Anna, also finds time to run this cosy little inn. La Casa Grande is made up of three village houses and an old stable block which have been linked together to create an organic, interesting and supremely welcoming inn. The atmosphere is far more that of home than hotel. There is a beautiful lounge up beneath the eaves with masses of books, plants and a view over the village rooftops. Downstairs is another lounge, a bar area and more plants and books. Rugs add warmth and colour to the traditional tile floors, a hammock awaits you at siesta time. La Casa Grande's bedrooms vary in size and configuration, mixing antique with modern furniture and they have bright bedspreads and simple bathrooms. Only breakfast is served but there is a fantastic tapas bar next door. Try the *montaditos*.

To see and do: bird-watching and walking in the Natural Park of Los Alcornocales, the Tarifa beaches, and day trips to Morocco by boat or hydro-foil

HOSTAL CASA DE LAS PIEDRAS

MAP: 10

Calle las Piedras 32
11610 Grazalema

Tel: 956 132014 or 956 132323 **Fax:** 956 132014

e-mail: info@casadelaspiedras.net

Web Page: www.casadelaspiedras.net

Closed: Never

Bedrooms: 2 Doubles and 14 Twins (all en suite), 16 rooms sharing bathrooms/toilets and 6 village Apartments

Price: Double/Twin €42.50, Double/Twin sharing €20
house for 2 €45, including VAT

Meals: Breakfast €6, Lunch/Dinner €9 including wine

Getting there: From Ronda take the C-339 towards Sevilla. Pass the Venta La Vega and shortly afterwards turn left to Grazalema. Here in the main square turn sharp right and head up the street to the left of the Unicaja bank. Casa de las Piedras is on the right after about 150m.

Management: Rafael & Katy Lirio Sánchez

It's been almost twenty years since I first stayed at Las Piedras and this simple hostal seems to get better and better as the years go by. It's long been popular with walking groups from the UK who base themselves here in the sure knowledge that a comfortable bed, good country cooking and a friendly welcome are guaranteed. The *hostal* is just up from the main square. Its whitewashed façade with old wrought-iron window grilles and two fine portals give it a rather grand look. You'll be greeted with a smile by Katy and Rafael (who also works as a taxi driver and can run you to the starting point of local walks). The best bedrooms are in the new wing of Las Piedras. Try to book one on the top floor. These are quieter and two of them manage to grab a view out across the village's terracotta rooftops. The rooms in the older part of Las Piedras are much more basic and share bathrooms and toilets (although the plan is to renovate this part in the coming year). In spite of the growing numbers of visitors, and the coach parties that arrive at the weekends, Grazalema is still worth a detour and the walking here is magnificent.

To see and do: walking in Grazalema Park, a visit to the blanket factory in the village centre, and visits to other white villages

MÁLAGA PROVINCE

HOTELS 047 TO 093

Rooftops of Benadalid

EL HORCAJO

MAP: 10

Ctra Ronda-Zahara de la Sierra km 95.5
29400 Ronda

Tel: 95 2184080 **Fax:** 95 2184171

e-mail: info@elhorcajo.com

Web Page: www.elhorcajo.com

Closed: Never

Bedrooms: 1 Single, 1 Double, 14 Twins and 10 Duplex rooms sleeping up to 4

Price: Single €50-62, Double/Twin €60-75, Duplex €67-133 + 7 % VAT

Meals: Breakfast included, Lunch/Dinner €15 excluding wine

Getting there: From Ronda take the A-376 towards Sevilla. After approximately 15km turn left at signs for Grazalema. Don't take the next left turn for Grazalema, but rather continue on towards Zahara. El Horcajo is signposted to the left of the road. Follow a long track down to the farm in the floor of the valley.

Management: Luis González

It's amazing how many small hotels have opened in the Ronda mountains in the past three or four years—evidence of the growing numbers of visitors to the area and of the substantial grants that have poured in from Brussels. El Horcajo was once a lowly cattle farm but has been given a new role in life thanks to the dynamism of owner Luis González. You reach the farm by winding down to the bottom of a deep valley that lies on the northern boundary of the Grazalema Natural Park. Heavy wooden doors lead into the huge, vaulted lounge (the former cattle byre). Just off to one side is the beamed dining room where simple, country-style cuisine is the key. Every last corner of the place has been decorated in traditional Andalusian rustic style with beams and terracotta floor tiles, cobbled courtyard, and wooden Ronda-style bedroom furniture. The quietest of the rather spartan bedrooms give onto the inner patio where a huge mulberry provides welcome shade in summer. The rooms in a newly added annex are mezzanine style, great for a family. Ronda and Grazalema are within easy driving distance.

To see and do: walking in the Grazalema Natural Park, visits to Ronda and the white villages, and the Pileta Cave

CORTIJO PUERTO LLANO

MAP: 10

Ctra Ronda la Vieja km 224
29400 Ronda

Tel: 95 2114227 **Fax:** 95 2114227

e-mail: cortijoronda@yahoo.es

Web Page: www.andalucia.com

Closed: Never

Bedrooms: 1 Single and 3 Twins

Price: Single €54, Twin €84 including VAT

Meals: Breakfast €6, no Lunch/Dinner available. There is plenty of choice in Ronda which is just 15 minutes from Puerto Llano.

Getting there: From Ronda take the A-376 towards Sevilla. After 9km turn right on the MA-449 towards Ronda La Vieja. The road climbs and then levels. The entrance to Cortijo Puerto Llano is on the right, next to marker post km 8.

Management: Aart van Kruiselbergen & Michael Cox

Cortijo Puerto Llano sits high on a hilltop above Ronda, a short walk from the Roman ruins of Acinipo whose theatre, hewn out of solid rock, is simply amazing yet curiously attracts few visitors. Aart and Michael have lived a long time in Spain. Both are artists and it's easy to see why they would have fallen in love with Puerto Llano, with its whitewashed walls, contrasted by the fields of wheat and sunflowers that grow right up to the house. It has been decorated with an artist's eye for detail. It is simple and elegant with a minimum of clutter and, of course, there are masses of paintings and drawings. A large guest lounge, reached by way of paths flanked by clipped hedges of rosemary, doubles as a gallery for Aart and Michael's work. The bedrooms, giving onto the cobbled inner patio, are also brightened by their paintings. You couldn't hope to meet with kinder hosts and although only breakfast is on offer, Ronda is just 15 minutes away. There is also a fully-equipped kitchen if you prefer to prepare your own meals.

To see and do: Roman theatre of Acinipo, Ronda, the white villages, and Setenil de las Bodegas

EL TEJAR

MAP: 10

Calle Nacimiento
29430 Montecorto

Tel: 95 2184053 **Fax:** 95 2184053

e-mail: eltejar@mercuryin.es

Web Page: www.sawdays.co.uk

Closed: July & August

Bedrooms: 2 Twins, I Double and 1 Double with own lounge

Price: Twin/Double €65, Double with lounge €70, or whole house rental approx. €950 weekly

Meals: Breakfast €5, Packed Lunches €7, Dinner €22.50 including aperitif, wine and coffee

Getting there: From Ronda take the A-376 towards Sevilla to Montecorto. As you arrive in the village, take a cobbled track sign-posted 'Bar La Piscina' (to the right of the *Ayuntamiento*). At the end of the track turn right, pass to the left of house No.54. Pass 2 more houses then go sharp right up the track and through the pines. Bear right to El Tejar.

Management: Guy Hunter-Watts

How do you describe your own home with any degree of objectivity? I'll have a go. El Tejar is the highest house in Montecorto, festooned with bougainvillaea, honeysuckle and jasmine with a sweeping panoramic view of mountains, wheat fields and forest. The interior design and décor evokes Andalusia's Moorish past. There are pointed arches, bright Moroccan *kilims* and deep ochre colour washes. The bedrooms are big with gorgeous views and really comfortable beds. Guests who stay here are treated like friends. You can help yourself to drinks from the bar, browse through hundreds of books on Spain or put on a CD. The sound of a spring-fed pool lulls you at siesta time whilst at breakfast *flamenco*, *fado*, jazz, blues or baroque music accompanies freshly-squeezed orange juice and potfulls of coffee. Many of our guest are walkers. I've written a walking guide to the area and have masses of suggestions for great routes. Having lived here for more than fifteen years, I know all of the best bars and restaurants in the area. But, best of all, my eversmiling Spanish housekeeper Paqui helps make a stay with us a truly southern Spanish experience. And her cooking is *ricísimo*.

To see and do: walking in the Grazalema Natural Park, visits to the Roman theatre of Acinipo, the Pileta Cave, Ronda and white villages

CORTIJO LAS PILETAS

MAP: 10

Ctra Antigua de Montejaque km 0.5
29400 Ronda

Tel: 605 080295

e-mail: cortijolaspiletas@hotmail.com

Web Page: www.andalucia.com/laspiletas

Closed: Never

Bedrooms: 3 Doubles and 4 Twins

Price: Double/Twin €80 including VAT and breakfast

Meals: Breakfast included, Dinner (on request only) €20

Getting there: Take the A-376 from Ronda towards Sevilla. After km post 107 take the left turn towards Montejaque. Las Piletas has red windows and is the first farm on the left.

Management: Elisenda Vidal Riba & Pablo Serratosa

Las Piletas is only a short drive from Ronda but is deeply bucolic. Elisenda and Pablo have breathed new life into the farm by converting the outbuildings of this traditional Andalusian *cortijo* into seven superbly comfortable guest bedrooms. These look out to a marvellous sweep of farmland where Pablo has marked walking routes and has built hides for bird watching. As well as raptors there are a host of other feathered things to be seen. The main farm building houses a delightful dining room where dinner feels like a real celebration. The atmosphere is intimate, the tables beautifully dressed and the food and wine first class (a larger restaurant is planned for next door). Also in the main farm building is a large lounge with comfy chairs and sofas, a perfect place to hunker down with a good novel. It is wonderful to sit in the evening and contemplate the changing light on the hillsides from the bedroom terraces, perhaps watching the *retinto* cattle returning home for the night. You are just a quarter of an hour from Ronda.

To see and do: ornithological routes, Ronda and the white villages, walking in the Grazalema park

LA FUENTE DE LA HIGUERA

MAP: 11

Partido de los Frontones
29400 Ronda

Tel: 95 2114355 **Fax:** 95 2114356

e-mail: info@hotellafuente.com

Web Page: www.hotellafuente.com

Closed: Never

Bedrooms: 3 Twins, 7 Suites & 1 Suite for 4

Price: Twin €130, Suites for 2 €160-189,
Suite for 4 €250 + 7% VAT

Meals: Breakfast included, Light lunches €15,
Dinner €35 excluding wine

Getting there: Take the A-376 from San Pedro de Alcántara, by-passing Ronda towards Sevilla. Shortly past the turning for Benaoján (don´t take this road!) between km posts 117 and 116, turn right. Go under a bridge and then turn left at the first fork. Cross a small bridge and after about 200m turn left again at the sign for the hotel.

Management: Christina & Pom Piek

When Pom and Tina decided to head south from Holland and convert a tumble-down olive mill, everyone else was opting for the Andalusian country style. But they were after something spicier, something different. So whole floors were shipped in from the Far East, there's not a twisted beam in sight and, where others might have hung a print of the Ronda bridge, there's modern art from Amsterdam. What they've achieved is a light, airy, exceptionally soothing series of spaces that are imbued with the laid-back spirit of the owners. The travel magazine *Condé Nast* seemed to get a finger on the pulse of the place when they wrote about the "chilled-out, house-party atmosphere". The hotel stands high on a hill surrounded by a vast olive grove with views out across the pool to Ronda. At night it is simply magical. The bedrooms (most of them suites) are huge, and the colonial-style furniture is nicely contrasted against the rooms' clean lines. The set-menu dinners are good, the selection of wines excellent and the hotel has a growing number of loyal clients, so be sure to book early.

To see and do: riding and walking in the Grazalema and Sierra de las Nieves Natural Parks, ballooning near Ronda, visits to Ronda town and the white villages

ARRIADH HOTEL

MAP: 11

Camino de Laura-Ronda
Apartado de Correos 490
29400 Ronda

Tel: 607 192 384

e-mail: arriadh@vodafone.es

Web Page: www.andalucia.com/arriadh

Closed: Never

Bedrooms: 4 Doubles and 1 Twin

Price: Double/Twin with terrace €65-75, Double/Twin with balcony €55-65 including breakfast & VAT

Meals: Breakfast included, light lunches approx €14,
Dinner €17 excluding wine

Getting there: From Ronda, at the roundabout on the ring-road, take the A-357 towards Campillos. After 200m turn left towards Arriate on the M-428. After 4km (just before arriving in Arriate) turn right and go up the hill. Go right again and follow the track to hotel.

Management: Ulrika Waldenström & Eduardo Tataje

The valley that leads north from Ronda towards Arriate is fast being populated by ex-pats in search of the 'Good Life'. Eduardo and Ulrika, on the run from the Swedish winters, found a spectacular location to build the small hotel of their dreams. It's on a high hillside which looks out across a verdant valley to the distant peaks of the Grazalema mountains. 'Small is beautiful' was their starting point. So they built just five, big bedrooms rather than trying to squeeze in a couple more and cramp their style (and that of their guests). The building's base elements are *andaluz* to the core: wafer bricks, terracotta tiles, locally made appliqué lamps and really attractive wooden furniture. Beds are big, bathrooms too, and central heating throughout the building is a real plus in winter when cold winds blow down the valley. Both rooms and food are really good value compared to hotels of a similar specification. Ulrika takes time and care when preparing suppers and her set menus have a higher-than-usual salad and fish content. A friendly, comfortable small hotel which, along with its newly planted garden, will grow in charm.

To see and do: Ronda, the white villages of the Grazalema Park, Ronda La Vieja and Setenil

FINCA LA GUZMANA

MAP: 11

Ctra El Burgo km 4
29400 Ronda

Tel: 610 826 279 or 600 006305

e-mail: info@laguzmana.com

Web Page: www.laguzmana.com

Closed: Never

Bedrooms: 3 Doubles and 4 Twins

Price: Double/Twin €55-65 including VAT

Meals: Breakfast included, Packed lunches on request €5

Getting there: From San Pedro de Alcántara take the A-376 to Ronda, then continue through town towards Sevilla. At the round-about with the traffic lights, take the first exit towards El Burgo. Go under the aqueduct and at km 4 (opposite the small restaurant La Venta) turn left down a sandy track. La Guzmana is on the left after 300m.

Management: Claire Casson & Peter MacLeod

La Guzmana, surrounded by olives and vines, stands on a high plateau a couple of miles north of Ronda. You may possibly have heard of the place in spite of the fact that it only recently opened its doors to paying guests. Peter and Claire were recently featured on *Sun, Sea and Scaffolding*, a TV series about Brits setting up businesses abroad. They worked hard to create their vision of the perfect small hotel (closely monitored by the cameras at times) sympathetically restoring then adding to their original 150 year old farm. The balustraded inner courtyard gives the place a definite *hacienda* feel while the decoration has stayed faithful to the local vernacular—beams, terracotta floor tiles and cheery tiles in the bathrooms. There is plenty of space in the bedrooms, lounge and dining rooms. The included breakfast is better than most, with free range eggs and in-season fruit from the farm. If you don't fancy driving into Ronda for supper, a friendly little *venta* can be found at the end of the lane.

To see and do: Ronda and the white villages, the Natural Parks of Sierra de la Nieves and Grazalema, the lakes of El Chorro

ALAVERA DE LOS BAÑOS

MAP: 11

Calle San Miguel s/n
29400 Ronda

Tel: 95 2879143 **Fax:** 95 2879143

e-mail: alavera@telefonica.net

Web Page: www.andalucia.com/alavera

Closed: December & January

Bedrooms: 1 Single, 8 Doubles and 2 Twins

Price: Single €50, Double/Twin €75, Double/Twin with
terrace €85 including VAT

Meals: Breakfast included, Lunch/Dinner €25-30 including wine

Getting there: From San Pedro take the A-376 to Ronda. Go
through the old town, cross the bridge and directly opposite the
Parador right into Calle Rosario. Take a right at the end, downhill to
the Fuente de los Ocho Caños. Turn left here and then take the first
right down a hill and cross the bridge to the Arab Baths. The hotel is
next door.

Management: Inmaculada Villanueva Ayala & Christian Reichardt

Alavera de los Baños literally means "by the side of the Arab Baths" and this small hotel stands cheek-by-jowel with what is probably Andalusia's best preserved *hammam* (arabic term for a bath house). When Christian and Inma, the hotel's young owners, first set eyes on the place, there was just a crumbling ruin here, but thanks to masses of hard work and the *savoir-faire* of a local architect, Alavera has become a favourite stopover whose popular restaurant's culinary slant is towards the flavours of North Africa. The decorative style of the dining room and the bedrooms is also evocative of Andalusia's Moorish past. *Kilims*, lamps and mosaic-topped tables were shipped in from the Maghreb and the colour washes are reminiscent of the earthy colours of that part of the world. Bedrooms are small but the space has been utilised imaginatively. Showers rather than baths and small sinks with handmade ceramic tiles are an attractive and practical space-saving solution. What you most remember about Alavera is the easy, relaxed manner of Christian and Inma who make a stay here doubly special.

To see and do: the Arab baths, the Plaza de Toros, La Casa del Rey Moro and La Mina

HOTEL SAN GABRIEL

MAP: 11

Calle Marqués de Moctezuma 19
29400 Ronda

Tel: 95 2190392 **Fax:** 95 2190117

e-mail: info@hotelsangabriel.com

Web Page: www.hotelsangabriel.com

Closed: 1-7 January, 21-31 July, 21-31 December

Bedrooms: 6 Doubles, 1 Twin, 6 'superior' Doubles and 3 Suites

Price: Double/Twin €70-82, 'superior' Doubles €80-92,
Suite €92-102 + 7% VAT

Meals: Breakfast €6.50, no Lunch/Dinner available. Several good
restaurants and tapas bars are very close to the hotel.

Getting there: From San Pedro de Alcántara take the A-376 to
Ronda. Take the first entrance into town. Pass in front of the old
town walls and then bear right and upwards into the old town. Here
take the second street on the left. The hotel is next to the Plaza del
Gigante. Leave bags then park. Hotel staff will help.

Management: José Manuel Arnal Pérez

The owners like to describe San Gabriel as *un pequeño gran hotel*, (a great little hotel). They're right. A stay here is somehow "greater" than the normal hotel experience. This exceptionally kind Ronda family makes you feel not only like an honoured guest but also like a friend of the family. I remember meeting a family who emerged from their room to find presents under the tree for them on Christmas day! The hotel is at the very heart of the old town of Ronda, just metres from that awesome gorge and bridge. This is every inch the grand, seigneurial townhouse—coat-of-arms above an entrance of dressed stone, wonderful old wrought-iron grilles wrapped about by a rampant honeysuckle, and a grand sweep of staircase (rescued from the old town hall) leading up to the bedrooms. There's the most inviting of lounges with masses of books, magazines, rugs, tapestries and family photos. Just beyond is a billiards room and a tiny "cinema" where you can watch one of your favourite oldies on DVD. The bedrooms are to write home about and there's a cellar bar for pre-dinner *tapas* and a *fino*. A very favourite address.

To see and do: the Mondragón Palace, El Puente Nuevo, La Casa del Rey Moro, and the cathedral of Santa María

LA CAZALLA

MAP: 11

Apartado de Correos 160
29400 Ronda

Tel: 95 2114175 or 678 456016 **Fax:** 95 2114175

Closed: Never

Bedrooms: 5 Doubles and 1 Suite

Price: Double €102-130, Suite €150-170 including breakfast
+ 7% VA, minimum stay 2 nights

Meals: Breakfast included, Lunch (Sunday only) €30,
Dinner €30 (Monday-Saturday but not Tuesday)

Getting there: Leave Ronda on the A-369 towards Gaucín. Go
through the traffic lights and at the second mini-roundabout turn right
at the sign 'Ermita Rupestre Virgen de la Cabeza'. After just 25m
(at a fork) go left and follow the blue dots on the stones for 2.8km
to La Cazalla.

Management: María Ruiz and Rodrigo Ashorn

Just to the south of Ronda the leafy Sijuela valley narrows to become a gorge of stunning natural beauty. Here, it seems, the romantic vision of Spain has suddenly been crystallised. María Ruiz was enchanted by an ancient farm at the mouth of the gorge and has created a small guest house with such sensitivity that the building seems to become one with its surroundings. La Cazalla's lounge would have any journalist purring— here is rock, light, a wonderfully sculptural hearth, masses of books and rugs—and a feeling of utter tranquility. The bedrooms, too, with an accent on deep comfort, are stylish but without pretensions and have wonderful mattresses and linen—an invitation for blissful repose. But La Cazalla's garden, crisscrossed by ancient water channels, is what I most remember. It is like an inventory of southern species and none of it has seen chemical fertilisers for decades. Add to this Rodrigo's imaginative cooking which looks to the best of things local, the proximity to Ronda, one of the most beautiful pools in Andalusia and you begin to get the measure of this wholly remarkable place.

To see and do: Ronda, the extraordinary 'Abanico' gorge, the Pileta caves and walks galore in the Natural Parks of Grazalema and Sierra de la Nieves

MOLINO DEL SANTO

MAP: 10

Barriada de la Estación s/n
29370 Benaoján

Tel: 95 2167151 **Fax:** 95 2167327

e-mail: molino@logiccontrol.es

Web Page: www.molinodelsanto.com

Closed: Early November - mid February

Bedrooms: 1 Single, 7 Doubles, 7 Twins and 3 Suites

Price: Double €80-132, Twin €92-150, Suite €112-176 including VAT. Half-board is obligatory during High Season.

Meals: Breakfast included, Half Board (lunch or dinner and afternoon tea) €24 per person per night

Getting there: From Ronda take the A-376 towards Sevilla, then go left on the MA-555 towards Benaoján. After 12km cross the railway and river bridges. Then turn left to Estación de Benaoján and follow the signs to El Molino.

Management: Pauline Elkin & Andy Chapell

Pauline Elkin and Andy Chapell have gradually built El Molino del Santo up to model small hotel status thanks to more than a dozen years of hard work and good will. The physical setting is magnificent—right beside a rushing mountain torrent that once powered the mill's waterwheels, surrounded by exuberant vegetation and with views out to the rocky hillsides of the Guadiaro valley. Guests return time and time again because of the friendliness of the staff and the reassurance of known-standards in El Molino's restaurant (one of the first in the area to make real efforts to buy organically-grown produce). In its bedrooms which are redecorated and improved at the end of every season. Andy and Pauline's hotel is the proof that ethics and business are happy bedfellows. Come here to walk, to visit Ronda and the white villages or just to relax beneath the willows to that wonderful sound of rushing water. But be sure to book your room as soon as possible; the word is already out about this magical world of shady corners, crystalline spring waters and solid comfort.

To see and do: the Pileta Cave, walking in the Grazalema Natural Park, visits to Ronda and the white villages

EL GECKO

MAP: 10

Calle Cañada Real del Tesoro
29391 Estación de Cortes de la Frontera

Tel: 95 2153315 **Fax:** 95 2153266

e-mail: elgecko@mercuryin.es

Web Page: www.hotelelgecko.com

Closed: December, January & February

Bedrooms: 5 Twins/Doubles

Price: Double/Twin €78 including VAT

Meals: Breakfast included, Lunch/Dinner €20-25 including wine

Getting there: From Ronda take the A-376 towards Sevilla, then left to Benaoján. Pass through the village, then go left towards Cortes de la Frontera. As you arrive in Cortes take a sharp left turn signposted for Gaucín and go downhill to Estación de Cortes. El Gecko is signposted to the right just before you cross the river.

Management: Rachel Dring

Rachel Dring managed the Casablanca restaurant in Gaucín for several years before opening her own small hotel right next to the river in the sleepy, railroad village of Estación de Cortes. She is brilliantly suited to her role of host—relaxed, caring and with the ability to make her staff feel a valued part of the big picture, one of the secrets of making a success of any small hotel. She also has a designer's feel for colour and composition. The hotel's gecko motif is her work and seems to reflect the optimistic, cheerful mood of the place. Much of its intimacy and high feel-good factor comes from the warm creamy-lemon colour scheme which is nicely contrasted by dark beams and lime-coloured chairs in the dining room and by richly-coloured bedspreads and cushions in the bedrooms. Four of the five large bedrooms look towards the river as does the dining room. Breakfast at El Gecko includes fresh fruit salads and delicious local bread whilst lunches and dinners are a fusion of flavours from the world over, with some great vegetarian options.

To see and do: walking in the Alcornocales and Grazalema Natural Parks, visits to the Pileta Cave, Ronda and the white villages

HOTEL RURAL BANU RABBAH

MAP: 10

Calle Sierra Bermeja s/n
29490 Benarrabá

Tel: 95 2150288 or 95 2150144 **Fax:** 95 2150005

e-mail: hotel@hbenarraba.es

Web Page: www.hbenarraba.es

Closed: Never

Bedrooms: 12 Twins

Price: Twin €57 + 7% VAT

Meals: Breakfast €3, Lunch/Dinner €10 including wine

Getting there: From Estepona take the N-340 towards Algeciras, then right via Manilva to Gaucín. From here go right towards Ronda on the A-369. After 4.5km, turn right down the hill to Benarrabá. The hotel is at far end of village next to the municipal pool.

Management: Jesús García

Although Benarrabá is just a couple of miles from Gaucín, few foreigners visit the village and there are just a handful of ex-pat residents. Yet this is an archetypical white village with gorgeous views out across the chestnut and oak forests of the Genal valley. At the far side of the village, alone on a spur next to the municipal sports ground, Hotel Banu Rabbah is beginning to establish a reputation amongst the walking community as a friendly, comfortable and very well-priced sleep-over. Although the building would win no prizes for its architecture, plants soften its angular lines. Half of the bedrooms, and the lounge/reception area, look out across the valley. The bedrooms are decorated with hand-painted wooden beds, tables and dressers and have large, arched terraces. The hotel's restaurant, which is just 25 metres from the main building, next to the village swimming pool, is not a venue for a gourmet extravaganza but rather for simple dinners which look to the local recipe books for their inspiration. The staff are young and friendly and the walking here is fantastic.

To see and do: walking in the Genal Valley, visits to the Pileta Cave, Gaucín and Ronda and the white villages

LA FRUCTUOSA

MAP: 10

Calle Convento 67
29480 Gaucín

Tel: 617 692784 **Fax:** 95 2151580

e-mail: lafructuosa@yahoo.es

Web Page: www.lafructuosa.com

Closed: Never

Bedrooms: 3 Doubles and 2 Twins

Price: Double/Twin €88 including VAT

Meals: Breakfast €4, Dinner €28-30 including wine. The restaurant is open May-October most days of the week. Check with the hotel.

Getting there: From Estepona take the N-340 towards Cádiz then go right via Manilva to Gaucín. Here turn right at the first junction and follow this street into the village. La Fructuosa is on the right just before you come to a small square and a *farmácia*.

Management: Luis and Jesús

Ask any of Guacín's ex-pat community where best to eat in the village and they invariably answer "La Fructuosa". Its cuisine looks to the 'Med' for inspiration and to whatever is in season for its ingredients. You might be served dolmas, tapenade or hummus as an apéritif, followed by an excellent *ibérico* (Iberian) sirloin steak or a kebab with Moroccan-style spices. Luis and Jesús are easy, cosmopolitan hosts who have shown enormous sensitivity in the restoration of this former *lagar* (a place where wine was made), preserving whatever they could of the original building whilst introducing bold colours (made with natural pigments brought from as far afield as Egypt and Tunisia) and modern decorative elements. The restaurant doubles as a gallery for local artists. There are five bedrooms and a guest lounge on the top two floors. Their decoration was a labour of love. There are handmade ceramic tiles and polished stucco in the bathrooms, ragged and sponged paint finishes, cut flowers, rugs from Tunisia and Afghanistan. Stay here and you'll bless the day your host's car broke down and they were forced to make an unscheduled stop in Gaucín.

To see and do: walking in the Gaucín area, day trip to Tangier, visits to Ronda and the white villages

HOTEL CASABLANCA

MAP: 10

Calle Teodoro de Molina 12
29480 Gaucín

Tel: 95 2151019 **Fax:** 95 2151019

Web Page: www.andalucia.com/hotelcasablanca

Closed: 1 November - mid March

Bedrooms: 2 Singles, 4 Doubles, 3 Twins and 2 Junior Suites

Price: Singles €55, Double/Twin €80-92,
Junior Suite €105 including VAT

Meals: Breakfast €7, Lunch €20 including wine/Dinner €25
including wine. The restaurant is closed on Mondays and at
lunchtime on Sunday.

Getting there: From Estepona take the N-340 towards Cádiz then
right via Manilva to Gaucín. Here (opposite the petrol station) turn
right into the village to the small square by a *farmácia* (which will be
on your right). The hotel is signposted. Park anywhere here then ask
a local the way to Casablanca!

Management: Susan & Mike Dring

The naming of this hotel was inspired. This is, indeed, a white village house, and a genuine *casa blanca*. From here there are incredible views of Morocco (even if you can't quite see as far as the town that Bogart and Bergman made famous). This enormous village house started life as a *bodega*, then later was given a much grander air when it became the home of a Spanish *marquesa*. She shipped in an amazing bannistered staircase, raised ceilings, added stucco mouldings and parquet floors and brought mirrors all the way from Venice (which are still in place today). You enter via a light and airy dining room where a Belgian chef has carned a reputation amongst the local ex-pats for excellent, imaginative cuisine. Try his *magret* of duck in cherry sauce, *gratin* of tiger prawns or chocolate pudding. There is a covered patio where you eat during the warmer months which looks out across a second patio and pool. Most bedrooms are wrapped round these patios and two of them grab that amazing view south. If you plan to stay at Casablanca be sure to book early. Mike and Sue's hotel is deservedly hugely popular.

To see and do: walking in the Gaucín area, the Pileta cave, visits to Ronda and the white villages

EL NOBO

MAP: 10

Apartado de Correos 46
29480 Gaucín

Tel: 95 2151303 **Fax:** 95 2117207

e-mail: spirit@mercuryin.es

Web Page: www.elnobo.co.uk

Closed: July & August

Bedrooms: 1 Double and 1 Twin

Price: Double €118, Twin €112 including breakfast & VAT

Meals: Breakfast included, no other meals served but plenty of choice in village of Gaucín

Getting there: From Estepona take the A-7 (toll highway) towards Algeciras. Take the first exit (after just 5 km) for Casares/Gaucín. Arrving in Gaucín, turn right (opposite the petrol station) into the village to a small square by a *farmácia* (on your right). Here turn the car round and follow a narrow road down past La Fructuosa restaurant. El Nobo is to the left of the track, 1km down this road.

Management: Sally and Christopher Von Meister

You'll need to travel a very long way to find as magnificent a setting as this. El Nobo straddles a hilltop just beneath Gaucín with views that defy description. Be here at sunset and you'll understand why this is one of the most photographed houses in Andalusia. Sally and Christopher told me that the most common reaction of new-arrivals when faced with the view down to Gibraltar and to the mountains of North Africa is simply an awe-inspired "wow!" The interior design and décor sets all of the journalists purring. *Condé Nast, The Sunday Times,* and *Casa y Campo* have all waxed lyrical reviews about the country-style furnishings, beautiful colour washes and the stunning garden that has been sculpted amongst the natural rock. Breakfast is a big, generous affair and it's hard to pull youself away from El Nobo's beautiful terrace. You are very close to the village and its many bars and restaurants and there are fantastic walks straight out from the house.

To see and do: walking in the Gaucín area, visits to Ronda and the white villages, day trip to Tangier

LA ALMUÑA

MAP: 10

Apartado de Correos 20
29480 Gaucín

Tel: 95 2151200 **Fax:** 95 2151343

Web Page: www.andalucia.com

Closed: Never

Bedrooms: 2 Singles, 3 Doubles, 1 Twin and 1 Apartment for 4

Price: Single €55, Double/Twin €110,
Cottage for 4 people €850 per week + 7% VAT

Meals: Breakfast included, Dinner €30 including wine

Getting there: From Estepona take the N-340 towards Algeciras then go right via Manilva to Gaucín. Here turn left at the first junction. Turn left again at the petrol station on the A-369 towards Algeciras. At km 44.8 turn left at the round post into 'La Almuña' estate. It is the house to the right of the track, behind a line of cypress trees.

Management: Diana Paget

There is nowhere to stay in Spain quite like La Almuña, one of the few B&Bs that really does live up to the Spanish dictum of *mi casa es tu casa* (my home is your home). The life and soul of the place is Diana Paget. Hers is a relaxed, shambolic and utterly welcoming home of the take-us-as-you-find-us type. Swallows nest in the kitchen, dogs lounge on the sofas, friends pop in and out for a cup of tea, a gin and tonic, or for dinner, and Diana manages to carry on with her culinary preparations unperturbed, the complete antithesis of the Forté Junior Manager. La Almuña was the main farmhouse on a large estate which is now shared by a number of (mostly British) families. From here there are incredible views out over the rolling farmlands south of Gaucín and to the distant Moroccan Rif. Although parts of the house are getting a little worn at the edges, guests return year after year to stay with Diana. They come to ride, walk, eat and converse, all in the very best of company.

To see and do: walking and riding in the Gaucín area, train ride to Ronda, the Tarifa beaches, and the Roman ruins at Bolonia

CORTIJO EL PUERTO DEL NEGRO

MAP: 10

Carretera de Colmenar km 1.8
29480 Gaucín

Tel: 95 2151239 or 649 011362 **Fax:** 95 2151239

e-mail: puertodelnegro@mercuryin.es

Web Page: www.karenbrown.com

Closed: 1 November - 1 March

Bedrooms: 2 Doubles, 2 Twins and 4 Cottages (self-catering)
with their own pools

Price: Double/Twin €164-184 + 7% VAT. Prices for cottages are
available on request.

Meals: Breakfast €12, Lunches €20-30 excluding wine,
Dinner €30 excluding wine. The restaurant is closed on Tuesdays.

Getting there: From Málaga take the N-340 and then the E-15
motorway towards Cádiz. Exit for Gaucín/Casares. Arriving in
Gaucín, go left at the first junction then left again at the petrol station
on the A-369 towards Algeciras. After 2km turn right at the sign for
Puerto del Negro. The hotel is on the left after 1.8km.

Management: Christine & Tony Martin

You may have read about El Puerto del Negro in a magazine or a newspaper somewhere on your travels. Journalists are invariably moved to hyperbole by this exceptional place and so, too, are those lucky enough to stay here. Its location is simply out of this world—a lone perch on a last spur of the Ronda Sierra with vast views out across forests and valleys to Gibraltar and Africa. A long drive arcs up to the hotel's white frontage, its lines softened by rambling creepers, wistaria and jasmine. Luscious gardens spill down from the surrounding terraces. Guests come for the utter tranquility and the exclusive house-party atmosphere in which the accent is placed firmly on the *better things in life*. The food at El Puerto del Negro is as cosmopolitan and as refined as the house itself. Bedrooms have every creature comfort and, like the lounge, mix furnishings and decorative elements from Africa, India and the Far East with a hint of the Home Counties. There's a snooker room, a tennis court and a pool placed at a discrete distance from the main house.

To see and do: train ride to Ronda, the villages of Genalguacil and Castellar, walking in the Gaucín area

HACIENDA LA HERRIZA

MAP: 10

Ctra Gaucín - El Colmenar km 6
29480 Gaucín

Tel: 951 068200 **Fax:** 951 068219

e-mail: reservas@laherriza.com

Web Page: www.laherriza.com

Closed: Never

Bedrooms: 17 houses sleeping 2, 4 or 6

Price: House with 1 bedroom €63-79, House with 2 bedrooms €102-126, House with 3 bedrooms €142-174 + 7% VAT

Meals: Breakfast included, Lunch/Dinner €18-24 including wine

Getting there: From Málaga take the N-340 and then the E-15 motorway towards Cádiz. Exit for Gaucín/Casares. Arriving in Gaucín go left at the first junction then left again at the petrol station on the A-369 towards Algeciras. After 2km turn right at the sign for Colmenar. The hotel is on the right after 6km.

Management: Heather Peyper and Carlo Carro García

La Herriza is hidden away in the forests that lie between Gaucín and its tiny railway station, El Colmenar. This is a place for folk who like to get well off the beaten track and the individual houses that make up this complex are ideal if you really value your privacy. There are seventeen houses which have been designed and decorated with a maximum of comfort in mind. All of them have phones and TVs, attractive carved 'Ronda-style' furniture which is nicely complement- ed by warm colour washes, coco matting and pretty stencilling. The restaurant and bar are in an adjacent building where huge glass windows let in the light and a wonderful view out across the surrounding cork oaks and almond groves. Since Heather and Carlo took the reins of La Herriza really good things have been happening in the kitchen. Barbecued meats are the specialty, deserts are fantas- tic (choc-aholics, don't miss the *soufflé de chocolate*) and the menu constantly changes following the dictates of the season. Carlo is one of the kindest, most charming hoteliers you could hope to meet

To see and do: the Colmenar gorge, the valley of the river Genal and Ronda and the white villages

CORTIJO EL PAPUDO

MAP: 10

11340 San Martín del Tesorillo

Tel: 95 2854018 **Fax:** 95 2854018

e-mail: papudo@mercuryin.es

Web Page: www.andalucia.com/gardens/papudo

Closed: Never

Bedrooms: 4 Doubles and 7 Twins

Price: Double/Twin €64-70 including VAT

Meals: Breakfast included, no Lunch/Dinner available. Simple restaurants in village are just a short drive from farm.

Getting there: From Málaga take the N-340 west towards Cádiz. Leave the N-340 at km 133 then follow the CA-514 to Secadero. Here bear left towards San Martín del Tesorillo. Turn right just before you reach the River Guadiaro. Continue for 1.5km and then 200m after you begin to climb up the first hill, turn sharply left into the drive of El Papudo (signposted).

Management: Vivien and Michael Harvey

The small village of San Martín lies at the southern end of the Guadiaro valley, just a few miles inland from Sotogrande. The exceptionally mild, moist climate of this part of Andalusia means that subtropical species thrive and the village is surrounded by vast plantations of fruit trees. This fecund climate also explains the existence of a number of garden centres. The Harveys own one of the best of them and they recently restored and renovated the neighbouring *cortijo* (farm) to create a small country B&B. The gardens, as you'd expect, are fantastic and anyone with even a passing interest in things horticultural will love the symphony of colour and texture that Vivien and Michael have created from plants, trees and shrubs. When converting the old granary to create the bedrooms, they tried to change as little as possible. Lots of the original beams and tiles are still in place and the abundance of wood gives the rooms a warm and welcoming feel. This is a great choice if you're looking for a quiet place to really unwind and there are good restaurants only a short drive away.

To see and do: a visit to Castellar de la Frontera, dolphin watching out from La Linea or Gibraltar, beaches and birdwatching

CORTIJO LA VIZCARONDA

MAP: 10

Lista de Correos
29692 Sabinillas

Tel: 95 2113742 or 650 530914 **Fax:** 95 2113742

e-mail: info@vizcaronda.com

Web Page: www.vizcaronda.com

Closed: Never

Bedrooms: 2 Doubles, 2 Twins and 1 *casita*

Price: Double/Twin €120-150,
Casita €400-500 weekly including VAT

Meals: Breakfast included, no Lunch/Dinner available. There are loads of restaurants in Sabanillas and Manilva.

Getting there: From Estepona take the N-340 towards Algeciras. In Sabinillas turn right at the Campsa petrol station towards Manilva. Turn hard left just past the km 2 post, and then right after just 50m. Go down a narrow road into the valley, pass stands of bamboo then follow a concrete track up to the Vizcaronda.

Management: John Waddingham & Henry Were

John and Henry looked at virtually every property that was for sale along this part of southern Spain's coastal fringe before being shown the crumbling walls of an old wine *bodega*, high on a hill close to Manilva. They were hooked. Who wouldn't have been when faced with that view down to the Mediterranean and across to the Moroccan Rif? Seven years on, they have created a real home-away-from home, a wonderfully intimate hotel that manages to match its setting. Vizcaronda has been decorated with buckets of razzmatazz. There are rich colours, snazzy fabrics, lamps and tables from the Far East and stacks of antiques that once graced the coaching inn they left behind in England. The four bedrooms, reached by way of a long wafer-bricked corridor, also have a festive, almost theatrical feel—splendid fabrics, baldequin beds, arches, old prints and curios, and each with its own private terrace. Although John and Henry only pre-pare breakfasts, they join guests for drinks and canapés before dinner (there are masses of restaurants nearby). A hugely convivial house-party atmosphere awaits you at Vizcaronda.

To see and do: a visit to nearby Roman baths, day trips to Morocco and Gibraltar, beaches and watersports

AMANHAVIS HOTEL

MAP: 11

Calle del Pilar 3
29679 Benahavis

Tel: 95 2856026 **Fax:** 95 2856151

e-mail: info@amanhavis.com

Web Page: www.amanhavis.com

Closed: 8 January - 12 February

Bedrooms: 3 Doubles, 3 Twins and 3 Deluxe rooms

Price: Double/Twin €119-149, Deluxe rooms €149-179 + 7% VAT

Meals: Breakfast €11, Dinner €37.50 excluding wine & VAT. The restaurant is closed Sundays.

Getting there: From San Pedro take the N-340 towards Algeciras and then turn right for Benahavis. Follow the road all the way through the village. After it turns sharply right, continue 25m and turn left. Amanhavis is on your left.

Management: Burkhard Weber

Anyone living in the Marbella area will have heard of Benahavis. This attractive medieval village, reached by way of a spectacular gorge that cuts in from the N-340, is a popular gastronomic destination amongst locals, ex-pats and holidaymakers. They come to eat at one of the several restaurants that line its narrow streets. The owners of Amanhavis wanted to create something with a rather different feel, and thanks to their decorative flair and imagination their small hotel now numbers amongst Andalusia's most original places to stay. The bedrooms are an extraordinary flight of fantasy, each one of them with a different historical theme inspired by Spain's medieval period and with decoration to match. In the Astronomer's Observatory you can look up to the stars from your pillow; Sultan Boabdil's chamber feels like it's been plucked from *One Thousand and One Nights*; whilst the Catholic Kings' chamber has a more regal air. The rooms wrap round a romantic inner courtyard and plunge pool beside which you can feast on inspired, Mediterranean cuisine accompanied by a selection of both Spanish and international wines.

To see and do: golf, beaches, Benahavis, Puerto Banus and Marbella

HOTEL POSADA DEL CANÓNIGO

MAP: 11

Calle Mesones 24
29420 El Burgo

Tel: 95 2160185 **Fax:** 95 2160185

e-mail: reservascanonigo@telefonica.net

Web Page: www.posadadelcanonigo.net

Closed: 24 December

Bedrooms: 7 Doubles and 5 Twins

Price: Double/Twin €44-52 including VAT

Meals: Breakfast included, Lunch/Dinner €12 excluding wine

Getting there: From Marbella take the A-355 to Coín and from there the A-366 to El Burgo. Head for the village centre, signposted *casco urbano* and pick up the signs for the Posada del Canónigo. The hotel is on the right as you head up Calle Mesones.

Management: María Reyes

If you're heading up to Ronda from Málaga and don't mind the odd hairpin bend, be sure to take the inland route via El Burgo. After ~~cutting through the irrigated valleys around~~ oín you climb up to a much wilder, starker swathe of mountains where eagles ride the winds and where *bandaleros* once plied their trade. Nowadays it's unlikely you'll be held up by anyone, yet El Burgo still feels as though the 21st century has passed it by. If you enjoy old-fashioned hospitality, this immensely friendly, family-run *posada*—the fruit of the conversion of an 18th century village house—should be your first choice. The heart of the hotel is its wonderfully intimate dining room where, in the colder winter months (the best time to visit), a fire always burns and where you dine on simple, traditional country food. The framed cross-stitch, the low beams, and the unrendered walls feel plucked from another age. The bedrooms, many of which have views out to the mountains, feel just as authentic with their beams, lace curtains, antique beds and terracotta floors.

To see and do: walking in the Sierra de las Nieves Natural Park, horse-riding, visits to Ronda and the white villages

HOTEL CERRO DE HÍJAR

MAP: 11

Cerro de Híjar s/n
29109 Tolox

Tel: 95 2112111 **Fax:** 95 2112111

e-mail: cerro@cerrodehijar.com

Web Page: www.cerrodehijar.com

Closed: Never

Bedrooms: 7 Doubles, 7 Twins, 2 Junior Suites and 2 Suites

Price: Double/Twin €64-76.5, Junior Suite €76.5-89
Suite €89-10 + 7 % VAT

Meals: Breakfast €7, Lunch/Dinner €26 excluding wine

Getting there: From Marbella take the A-355 towards Coín. Take the first turn for Monda, go through the village, then take the MA-413 for Guaro. Pass Guaro and at the next junction go left on the A-366 towards Ronda, then left to Tolox. Follow the signs for *balneario* and here follow the signs up to the hotel.

Management: Guillermo González, Eugenio Llanos & Martín Jerez

What a position! If a 'room with a view' is your idea of hotel heaven then book a night or two at Cerro de Híjar. The hotel's perch, high above the spa village of Tolox, is simply breathtaking. From here you can see for kilometres across the rumpled mountains and gentler foothills of the Sierra de la Nieves. The hotel is managed by three friendly young Spaniards. One of them worked at one of the few Michelin-starred restaurants in southern Spain before bringing his culinary nous to Hijar. The food (*cocina gastronómica imaginitiva*) and its presentation are simply fantastic and the prices are much lower than you'd expect for food of this standard (you'd pay at least three times as much in London). The bedrooms are taste-fully put together, too. They have bright colour washes, Mexican furniture, Turkish wall-hangings, lots of modern art, and most rooms grab a glimpse of that wrap-around panorama. Cerro de Hijar is a superlatively tranquil yet bright and cheery place to stay where you absolutely must be sure to stay for dinner. The night skies, with so little light pollution, are truly amazing.

To see and do: walking in the Sierra de Nieves Natural Park, golf in Alhaurín, Ronda and the white villages

LA POSADA DEL ANGEL

MAP: 11

Calle Mesones 21
29610 Ojén

Tel: 95 2881808 **Fax:** 952 881810

e-mail: info@laposadadelangel.com

Web Page: www.laposadadelangel.com

Closed: 1-15 January

Bedrooms: 10 Doubles and 7 Twins

Price: Double/Twin €70-93, Double with
terrace €84-111 including VAT

Meals: Breakfast €6

Getting there: From Málaga take the N-340 towards Cádiz then exit
at signs for Marbella/Ojén. Take the A-355 to Ojén and here watch
for signs to the village centre. Park in the square.

Management: Frank Thomas

Wonderful Ojén! So pretty, so Andalusian and yet so close to the busy coast. You can only wonder why more ex-pats haven't chosen this place to buy their dream-home in the sun. Part of the reason, at least, is that the swathe of mountains surrounding the village has recently been declared a Unesco Biosphere Reserve, keeping the developers at bay. Should you visit the village, stay at the Posada del Angel, plum in the centre of this *pueblo blanco*. Its Breton owners, with masses of good taste and Gallic *savoir-faire* have fashioned a wonderful small hostelry from five tumble-down village houses. The spirit of the place was born of the owner's love of angels. She commissioned a remarkable series of paintings for the inn from Lorenzo Saval, a Málaga artist. Like his angel paintings, the Posada is a flight of fantasy, soaring high above the commonplace. Every room has a different mood but all exude warmth and personality, are beautifully finished and have superb beds and sparkling bathrooms. Perhaps most memorable of all is the balustraded patio with its carved columns from India and *mozarab* windows. Enchanting.

To see and do: the Natural Park of the Sierra de Juanar, the wine and olive oil museums in the village and beaches just 10 minutes away

LA HOSTERÍA DE DON JOSÉ

MAP: 11

Paseo del Nacimiento
29610 Ojén

Tel: 95 2881147 or 655 583210 **Fax:** 95 2881147

e-mail: hdonjose@jazzviajeros.es

Web Page: www.hdonjose.com

Closed: Never

Bedrooms: 2 Doubles, 2 Twins, 1 Triple and 1 Family room

Price: Double/Twin €54-70, Triple €80-90, Family room with balcony, sleeping 3 €90-105 including VAT

Meals: Breakfast included

Getting there: From the N-340 exit for Marbella/Ojén, then head north to Ojén on the A-355. Follow the signs to the Hostería which is at the very top of the village.

Management: Isabel Sánchez Márquez

I had the good fortune to happen upon La Hostería de Don José when visiting Ojén. My appetite was already whetted by the steep drive up to the *posada* which is at the very top of the village. The higher you climb, the more spectacular are the views down to the Mediterranean. You immediately warm to Isabel (she speaks English fluently) who welcomes you with the big smile that she wears throughout the day. She takes great pride in the small inn that she opened just five years back. Its base elements and decorative style are one hundred per cent *andaluz*—wafer brick and terracotta tiles without and, within, more modern tiles with carved wooden furniture and a cheery colour scheme. You sense Isabel's feminine hand in the smaller details like dried flowers, loads of knick-knacks, copper saucepans, local pottery, a rocking horse and *Lladro*-style figurines. The bedrooms are clean-as-clean can be and have stunning views across the village rooftops to the distant sea. I'd pay the extra to get one with a terrace. The whole place is imbued with Isabel's good nature and she is always around to help you plan your sorties.

To see and do: the wine museum and the old centre of Ojén, the Paseo de la Cueva walk, and beaches just 10 minutes away

HOTEL RESTAURANTE SANTA FE

MAP: 11

Ctra de Monda km 3
29100 Coín

Tel: 95 2452916 **Fax:** 95 2453843

e-mail: info@santafe-hotel.com

Web Page: www.santafe-hotel.com

Closed: Last 2 weeks in November and 2 weeks in January/February

Bedrooms: 5 Twins

Price: Twin €66 including VAT

Meals: Breakfast included, Lunch/Dinner approx. €27.50 including wine

Getting there: From Málaga take the N-340 towards Cádiz/Torremolinos. After just 200m turn right for Coín. Just before Coín take the A-355 towards Monda then turn right at km 17. Santa Fe is just after the T-junction on the left hand side of road. Turn left at the piles of white stones.

Management: Warden & Arjan van de Vrande

Santa Fe could be just the place to stay if you are wanting a sea and mountain holiday. You can be on the beach in just half an hour and the Sierra de las Nieves is right on your doorstep, too. The hotel, just to one side of the main road that cuts through the hills between Coín and Marbella, is an old farmhouse surrounded by the groves of citrus fruit that line the Guadalhorce valley. The focus of the place in the warmer months is the poolside terrace (where a huge olive tree provides welcome shade) whilst when temperatures drop a warmly decorated, beamed dining room is a wonderfully intimate spot for your meals. Foodies will enjoy Santa Fe. Its Dutch owners, Arjan and Warden, have built up a solid reputation for their mix of Andalusian and international food and lots of ex-pats drive up from the coast to eat here. Amongst the specialities are crayfish with spinach, sirloin of lamb *al vino de Jerez* and wonderful Dutch-style apple pie. The beamed, terracotta-tiled bedrooms are inviting, too, and have recently been completely redecorated.

To see and do: horse-riding, walking in the Sierra de la Nieves Natural Park, visits to Puerto Banus, Marbella and beaches

HACIENDA DE SAN JOSÉ

MAP: 11

Buzón 59, Entrerrios
29650 Mijas

Tel: 95 2119494 **Fax:** 95 2119404

e-mail: haciendasanjose@yahoo.co.uk

Web Page: www.hotelruralhaciendasanjose.com

Closed: 20 June - 31 August

Bedrooms: 5 large Twins (Junior Suites)

Price: Twin €140-160 + 7% VAT

Meals: Breakfast included, Dinner €20-25 excluding wine. The restaurant is closed Wednesday evenings.

Getting there: From Fuengirola take the N-340 towards Marbella. Leave the N-340 at Cala de Mijas Exit then follow the signs 'Campo de Golf'/'La Cala Golf'. Turn right at the first roundabout, then at the next fork turn right again towards Entrerrios. The hotel is signposted on the left after 1.8km.

Management: Nicky & José García

Nicky and José built and managed a successful tennis club before envisaging a more peaceful future in their own small country-house hotel. As past hoteliers and travellers, too, they knew exactly what they were after—a truly comfortable home-away-from-home in a peaceful and rural location yet still close to the Costa del Sol. As you follow the steep drive up to this *hacienda* style building, it's hard to imagine that a couple of years back this was a bare hillside. Oleander, cypress, olive, palm and plumbago are already taking root and a sea of colour laps up to the house's front door. The five guest rooms are set around a pebbled inner courtyard in which a fountain softly gurgles. It feels almost cloister-like. Your room will be huge, airy and light. Each room has its own terrace, an enormous bathroom, fitted wardrobes and top-of-the-range linen and mattresses. You won't sleep more comfortably than here. Up a level is a large lounge, a cosy library and a brightly decorated dining room. You eat well at San José and you won't want for good wine. José has a well-stocked cellar and enjoys sharing his knowledge of things oenological with his guests.

To see and do: nearby beaches, golf, visits to Mijas pueblo, Puerto Banus and Marbella

THE BEACH HOUSE

MAP: 11

Urbanización El Chaparral
Ctra de Cádiz N-340 km 203
29649 Mijas Costa

Tel: 95 2494540 **Fax:** 95 2494540

e-mail: info@beachhouse.nu

Web Page: www.beachhouse.nu

Closed: Almost never

Bedrooms: 8 Doubles and Suite

Price: Double €140, Suite €75 including VAT

Meals: Breakfast included, no Lunch/Dinner available. Lots of local and international restaurants are a short drive from The Beach House.

Getting there: From the airport take the N-340 towards Cádiz then go right onto the A-7. At the fork, follow signs for Fuengirola/ Mijas. Pass km post 202 and after approximately 600m exit for Cala de Mijas. Take the N-340 back towards Fuengirola. Immediately after the footbridge, exit on the slip road to The Beach House.

Management: Kjell Sporrong

After a recent change of owners and complete decorative metamorphosis, The Beach House now numbers amongst Andalusia's most stylish small hotels. Kjell worked in the world of design in Stockholm and every last corner of his Andalusian villa has been decorated with aesthetic appeal in mind. There's a hint of nineties minimalism, a definite debt to things Japanese and an overall feel of repose for body and mind in both the lounge-diner and in the bedrooms. The main protagonists here are the sea and the sky, their colours changing with each passing hour. The Mediterranean laps up to within metres of The Beach House and its pool and terrace almost seem to fuse with the ocean. The best rooms here are naturally those with sea views; the busy N-340 runs close to the other side of the house and you hear passing traffic from these back rooms. Kjell is a charming, and cosmopolitan host and prepares a wonderful buffet breakfast which will include a glass of chilled cava at the weekend. He will, of course, direct you towards the best local restaurants.

To see and do: watersports, beaches, horse-riding, golf, visits to Mijas pueblo and Marbella

HOSTAL MARBELLA

MAP: 11

Calle Marbella 34
29640 Fuengirola

Tel: 95 2664503 **Fax:** 95 2664503

e-mail: info@hostalmarbella.info

Web Page: www.hostalmarbella.info

Closed: Never

Bedrooms: 6 Doubles and 17 Twins nearly all with own bathrooms

Price: Double/Twin €39-59 including VAT

Meals: Breakfast €2.10

Getting there: From the airport take the N-340/E-15, then take
Exit 214 for Fuengirola. Head into the town centre. The *hostal* is
close to the *Policía Local*. Nearest parking is Aparcamiento Alfíl.

Management: Leif Malmborg

There is a real dearth of small, decent places to stay on the Costa del Sol. But if you're looking for a place close to the airport which is clean, quiet and friendly Hostal Marbella fits the bill. This simple *hostal* is at the heart of Fuengirola and guests who stay come from all over the world, including Spain. The rooms are 'safe' rather than memorable but that is what Lief, the amiable Swedish owner, set out to create. The only public space, as such, is a small guest lounge next to reception where there is a fridge full of cold drinks, plenty of literature on the area and where, if you like, a simple continental breakfast can be served. I, at least, would rather head off to one of the town's many *cafés* and have my coffee *al fresco*. Lief gives his guests a lot of his time and, like the rest of the staff, really wants you to get the most out of a stay in Fuengirola. As is the case with neighbouring Torremolinos there are still bars and restaurants in the town which are frequented predominantly by Spanish rather than foreigners. Be sure to book a room with a bathroom, well worth the extra few euros.

To see and do: beaches and watersports, golf courses and day trips to Mijas and other inland villages

LAS ISLAS

MAP: 11

Calle Canela Mimosa s/n
Urbanización Torreblanca del Sol
29640 Fuengirola

Tel: 95 2475598 **Fax:** 95 2464298

e-mail: ziziclo@terra.es

Web Page: www.costadelsol.spa.es/hotel/lasislas

Closed: Mid November - early March

Bedrooms: 4 Doubles and 6 Twins

Price: Double/Twin €75 + 7% VAT

Meals: Breakfast included, Dinner approx. €40 including wine. The restaurant is closed on Mondays.

Getting there: From the airport take the N-340 towards Algeciras. Bypass Torremolinos, continue on through Benalmádena Costa then Caravajal to Torreblanca. Here at a roundabout (just as you pass a Chemist's) turn right and follow the blue signs to the hotel.

Management: Ghislaine & Hardy Honig

Who would ever guess that places like this could exist less than a couple of kilometres from the sprawling development of Andalusia's bustling coast? Ghislaine's parents bought this tiny, hidden glade nearly 40 years ago when few people had heard of Fuengirola. A villa and rooms were built and a wonderful garden planted. Contemplating the jacaranda, date palms, cypress and banana trees, you feel as if you were on a tropical island. The 12 guest rooms look out onto all this greenery and one or two of them catch a view of the sea. Their decoration is fresh and simple—nothing fancy but then nothing's missing, either—and all of the rooms have balconies. You'll awake here to a chorus of birdsong rather than to the sound of a TV in the next room (in fact, there are no TVs here). But the heart and soul of Las Islas is its restaurant. Hardy's food is first-class, with a definite debt to things French and German, and you couldn't wish for a more charming hostess than Ghislaine who greets you with the kindest of smiles.

To see and do: golf, horse-riding, watersports, visits to Mijas Pueblo and Picasso museum in Málaga

EL MOLINO SANTISTEBAN

MAP: 11

A-366 km 52-53
Apartado de Correos 86
29100 Guaro

Tel: 95 2453748 or 687 679021

e-mail: info@hotelmolino.com

Web Page: www.hotelmolino.com

Closed: December-end February

Bedrooms: 3 Doubles and 3 Twins

Price: Double/Twin €65-75 + 7% VAT

Meals: Breakfast included, no Lunch/Dinner apart from vegetarian meals on Tuesday (for 6 or more guests) approx. €30

Getting there: From Málaga airport take the N-340 towards Cádiz and almost immediateley turn right at the signpost for Coín. Here take the A-366 towards Ronda. Molino Santisteban is just to the right of the road, between marker posts km 52 and km 53.

Management: Frits Blomsma

Frits and Gisele are amongst a growing number of young Europeans who have headed south in search of a better life in the hills of Andalusia. Visit them and you'll understand why they would have fallen for this old mill house situated just beside the road that cuts through the hills towards Ronda. It stands amongst groves of citrus and fields of almonds and avocados in the fertile valley of the Río Grande. Santisteban's architecture is rather reminiscent of a *hacienda* but on a smaller scale. The six bedrooms give onto a sheltered inner patio where a gurgling fountain and birdsong is about all that you'll hear at siesta time. The dining room, just across from the main building, offers cool respite during the hotter months and a cosy retreat in winter where you breakfast round a magnificent antique almond-wood table. Orange juice is always squeezed fresh from Santisteban's own fruit and there are cheeses and meats, jams and cereals, yoghurts and eggs to set you up for the day should you head out for a hike along the valley or venture up into the Serranía de las Nieves Natural Park. There are also two good restaurants just metres from the front gate.

To see and do: walking in the Sierra de las Nieves Natural Park, visits to Ronda and the white villages

HOTEL LA ERA

MAP: 11

Partido Martina
Los Cerrillos, parcela 85
29566 Casarabonela

Tel: 95 2112525 or 95 2112538 **Fax:** 95 2112009

e-mail: hotellaera@tiscali.es

Web Page: www.hotellaera.com

Closed: 22 December - 7 January

Bedrooms: 6 Doubles, 2 Twins and 1 Suite

Price: Double/Twin €115, Suite €135 including VAT

Meals: Breakfast €9, Dinner €25 excluding wine

Getting there: From the airport take the N-340 round Málaga then exit for Cártama/Universidad on the A-357. Bypass Cártama then exit on the MA-403 towards Casarabonela. Just before you reach the village turn right at the signs for La Era. Follow the signs for 2km to the hotel.

Management: Isabel Manrara Díaz

I had the good fortune to stumble upon La Era when heading home through the mountains east of Ronda. My hotel appetite is always whetted by any approach that promises to get me away from civilisation, and when I rounded a final bend and came up to La Era, high on a spur of the mountains across from beautiful Casarabonela, I sensed that this was going to be a memorable night away. Isabel and Frank left no stone unturned in their quest to create a truly special country hotel. Taps, beds, fabrics, mattresses, doors, sheets, towels are all are top-of-the-range and no detail has been forgotten by Isabel whose pride in her hotel is tangible—and justified. She also happens to be an exceptionally good cook and although I arrived unannounced she managed to conjure up a delicious meal in next-to-no-time (normally menus are discussed and tailored to your tastes). The extent of her breakfast buffet will have you forgetting about lunch. Add to all this a comfortable lounge, a friendly welcome and amazing views and you should begin to get a feel for the place.

To see and do: El Chorro lakes and gorge, the Sierra de las Nieves Natural Park and Ronda.

LA POSADA DEL CONDE

MAP: 11

Calle Barriada Conde del Guadalhorce 16-18
29550 Ardales

Tel: 95 2112411 or 95 2112800 **Fax:** 952 112805

Web Page: www.laposadadelconde.com

Closed: 2 weeks in January

Bedrooms: 1 Single, 24 Twins and 1 Suite

Price: Single €45, Twin €60, Suite €180 + 7% VAT

Meals: Breakfast €5, Lunch/Dinner €20 including wine

Getting there: From Málaga take the A-357 towards Campillos. Just past Ardales turn right at the sign 'Embalses Conde del Guadalhorce/ El Chorro'. Follow the road straight for 7km (ignoring the right turn for El Chorro). The hotel is on the right at the far end of a reservoir (after crossing the dam).

Management: Miguel Angel Gonzalez Rodríguez

The first time I stayed at La Posada del Conde I felt obliged to question the bill. Could it really be so ... little? The hotel's bedrooms are stylishly decorated, bathrooms are large, all of the fabrics and furnishings first class, yet their price tag is paltry compared to hotels of a similar standard in Andalusia—and this, in a magnificent swathe of mountain terrain. The hotel is next to the beautiful Guadalhorce reservoir where you can fish or swim and where you are very close to some spectacular walking country. (Sadly the extraordinary walkway along the side of the Chorro gorge, El Camino del Rey, has recently been closed.) The food at the Posada is good value, too. House specialties include stuffed sirloin of pork and lamb basted in honey. Or you could take an evening stroll along the edge of the reservoir and eat at El Kiosco, a restaurant that looks out across the reservoir. From here it's only an hour to the airport, making it an excellent place to begin or end a holiday in Spain. A small, friendly and reliable place to stay—and a personal favourite.

To see and do: the Chorro gorge, the Torcal Park and, in season, flamingo watching at the Laguna de Fuente Piedra

CASA RURAL DOMINGO

MAP: 11

Arroyo Cansino 4
29500 Álora

Tel: 95 2119744 **Fax:** 95 2119744

e-mail: casadomingo@vodafone.es

Web Page: www.casaruraldomingo.com

Closed: Never

Bedrooms: 1 Single, 1 Double, 1 Suite,
1 large Apartment and 2 Studios

Price: Single €39, Double €60, Suite €70,
Apartment €650 weekly, Studio €450 weekly including VAT

Meals: Breakfast included (although not for studios/apartment). No
Lunch/Dinner but good restaurants and tapas bars a short drive away
in Álora

Getting there: From Málaga take the A-357 towards Campillos via
Cártama. 16km after Cártama turn right towards Álora and follow the
signs for 'Álora Estación'. Cross the road at the T-junction and head
uphill on a good track for about 900m. Then go left to Casa Domingo.

Management: Cynthia & Domien Doms

Dom and Cynthia are another young couple who have migrated south to set up a small B&B in the mountains of Málaga. They used to run a bar in Belgium and are well used to coping with a constant stream of visitors. They manage to do so with a vitality and enthusiasm that is both genuine and infectious. They built the home of their dreams on a hillside above Álora, from where there are exhilarating views down across the town and to the mountains stretching west towards Ronda. The garden has been sculpted round a large pool and just to one side is a tennis court and boules pitch. The place would be great for a family holiday and there's a barbecue area that guests are welcome to use. Most of the year breakfast is served out on the terrace. Dom busies around helping to organise your day and, if you like, can help you search out your own dream home in the valley. There are several places where you can get a good dinner in Álora, and Casa Domingo is well-placed for trips to both the mountains and the coast.

To see and do: Álora, visits to the Ardales Natural Park, El Torcal Natural Park and Antequera

CORTIJO VALVERDE

MAP: 11

Apartado de Correos 47
29500 Álora

Tel: 95 2112979 **Fax:** 95 2112979

e-mail: cortijovalverde@mercuryin.es

Web Page: www.cortijovalverde.com

Closed: Never

Bedrooms: 3 Doubles and 4 Twins

Price: Double/Twin €84-96 + 7% VAT

Meals: Breakfast included, light snacks available at lunch time,
Dinner (Tuesday, Thursday and Sunday nights) €28 including apéritif

Getting there: From Málaga take the A-357 towards Campillos. Then
go right for Álora. Turn right at the junction and after 300m, turn left
for Álora. Cross the river and at the junction by bar 'Los Caballos' turn
left towards Valle de Abdalajasís. Pass km post 36, cross a small
bridge, pass an old bus shelter and then take the fork immediately to
the right. After 200m turn sharply left and uphill to Valverde.

Management: Moyra & Rod Cridland

Heading north from Álora towards the Torcal Park, you follow the narrowest of country roads that meanders its way through fields of wheat and groves of olives and almonds. You sense that you are headed for the heart of that much touted "real" Spain. When Rod and Moyra bought this small holding, there was just a tumble-down farmstead here but after many months of hard work they have seen its metamorphasis into a really comfortable country inn. Little remains of the old farm apart from the cobbled *era* (threshing circle) which, like the present house, catches the breezes that are blow down the valley. The most remarkable feature of Valverde is the enormous pool that lies between the main house and five of the guest rooms—20 lengths of this one and you'll have earned your supper. And an excellent supper it will be. Rod modestly describes his oven-based creations as "good, honest food" and he drives all the way to Antequera to buy fresh vegetables. His and Moyra's enthusiasm for their adopted country is refreshing and they are now even running intensive Spanish courses. Details of courses and of special Christmas and New Year breaks are available on request.

To see and do: visits to El Chorro gorge, the towns of Antequera, Álora, and Málaga, and El Torcal Natural Park

LA POSADA DEL TORCAL

MAP: 11

Partido de Jeva
29230 Villanueva de la Concepción

Tel: 95 2031177 **Fax:** 95 2031006

e-mail: hotel@eltorcal.com

Web Page: www.eltorcal.com/PosadaTorcal

Closed: December & January

Bedrooms: 1 Single, 2 'standard' Doubles, 6 'superior' Doubles, 1 Suite and 20 Cottages/Farmhouses

Price: Single €125, Standard Double €155, Superior Double €180, Suite €260 + 7% VAT. Prices for cottages/farmhouses on request

Meals: Breakfast included, Lunch/Dinner €35 excluding wine

Getting there: From Málaga take the N-331 towards Antequera. Take Exit 148 for Casabermeja/Colmenar. In Casabermeja turn right for Almogía and go left at the junction with signs for Villanueva de la C. Go uphill then left at the junction. After 1.5km go right at the signs for La Joya/La Higuera. The hotel is to the left of the road after 3km.

Management: Karen Ducker

If you like to really get away from it all yet prefer to do so without leaving your creature comforts behind, then the Posada del Torcal will be your type of place. What I most like about it are its heart-stopping views and the open-plan bedrooms that have raised corner tubs where you can soak away your troubles without missing a second of the amazing outdoor panorama before you. Beds are enormous, the decoration stylishly picks-and-mixes the modern with the traditional, and the terracotta tiled floors are underfloor heated. Hidden away in a rustic-style cabinet is satellite TV and video. Downstairs is a huge guest lounge and dining room and just beyond a swimming pool (heated in winter), a jacuzzi, a gym, an 'astroturf' tennis court as well as a sauna where you can (try to) pummel away those calories. The Torcal's food is excellent. There are wicked deserts, lots of vegetarian dishes and a good wine list. A hotel where the accent is very much on the 'Big Relax' but you should find time to explore the incredible weathered karst formations of the Torcal park.

To see and do: visits to El Torcal Natural Park, El Chorro gorge and lakes, the towns of Antequera and Fuente de la Piedra

CASA DE ELROND

MAP: 11

Barrio Seco s/n
29230 Villanueva de la Concepción

Tel: 95 2754091 **Fax:** 95 2754091

e-mail: elrond@mercuryin.es

Web Page: www.casadeelrond.com

Closed: Never

Bedrooms: 1 Double, 1 Twin and 1 Triple

Price: Double/Twin €49, Triple €68. Minimum stay 2 nights

Meals: Breakfast included, no Lunch/Dinner available, but some good, simple *ventas* a short drive away in Villanueva

Getting there: Round Málaga on the N-340 then take the N-331 towards Antequera/Granada. At km 241 exit for Casabermeja. Enter the village, go to the top of a hill and turn right at the junction with signs for Villanueva de la C. Here go left at the junction and continue 3km to the house which is signposted just to the right of the road.

Management: Una & Mike Cooper

You may well have heard of the Torcal Natural Park. This is Andalusia's answer to Capadocia, a huge limestone plateau which has been gradually weathered into the most phantasmagorical of shapes by the action of wind and rain. In its southern lee, just off to one side of one of the province's quietest roads, this tiny B&B has long been one of my favourite stopovers in the area, and proof that a good place to stay can also be a simple place to stay. Mike and Una welcome you with unaffected hospitality. Their guest house has just three small bedrooms but these are cosily furnished, sparkling clean and with comfortable beds. In short, they are worth every last euro of their modest price tag. This is a place where life tends to centre round the front terrace which has a massive panoramic view of the rumpled chains of mountains stretching down towards the Mediterranean. The sunsets here are unbelievable. Una no longer cooks evening meals but you'll find good food at Bar Durán or Diego's bar. Should you stay, be sure to visit the nearby El Chorro gorge.

To see and do: visits to El Chorro gorge and lakes, El Torcal Natural Park, and the town of Antequera

CORTIJO EL PERAL

MAP: 11

Finca Puerto El Peral
Monterroso
29150 Almogía

Tel: 952 430092 **Fax:** 952 430781

e-mail: puertoelperal@hotmail.com

Web Page: www.puertoelperal.com

Closed: Never

Bedrooms: 6 Doubles, 2 Twins and 2 Junior Suites

Price: Double/Twin €120-140, Junior Suite €140-160 + 7% VAT

Meals: Breakfast included, light lunches €8-17,
Dinner €35 excluding wine

Getting there: From Malaga take the ring road exit for Cártama on
the A-357. Exit from A-357 at km 64 for Campanillas. Go left at the
first junction, then the next right and after 50m (at a roundabout) go
left and follow the road to Almogía. Follow this road past the
village for 7km then go left. The farm is on the right after 2km.

Management: Heti Van der Pol & Alan Handforth

Head just an hour inland from Spain's populated southern coast and you find yourself in a different world. Almogía feels remote but in fact it's only half an hour from Málaga. Cortijo El Peral's hidden plateau, a few miles north west of the village, feels even further removed from 'civilisation'. Yet this place is 'civilised' in the best sense of the word. Alan and Heti have created a superbly comfortable *hacienda*-style hotel where the accents are on superb food and complete rest for body, mind and soul. The bedrooms are wonderful—massive with enormous beds ('super king-size'!), luxurious linen and towels. The views take you out across the farm's olive and almond groves. Begin an evening at El Peral with a drink at the bar with Alan who is an easy and amiable host whilst Heti works her culinary magic in a state-of-the-art kitchen. Her first source of inspiration is the Mediterranean, she's big on Italian and French dishes but, if the mood takes her, you may be offered a Thai meal. If you fancy something more ethnic, head down the quietest of country lanes to an excellent local *venta*.

To see and do: the Torcal Park, the old town of Antequera, horse riding and walking

HOTEL LARIOS

MAP: 4

Calle Larios 2
29005 Málaga

Tel: 95 2222200 **Fax:** 95 2222407

e-mail: info@hotel-larios.com

Web Page: www.hotel-larios.com

Closed: Never

Bedrooms: 3 Doubles, 31 Twins and 6 Suites

Price: Double/Twin €136 weekday or €111.5 weekend,
Suite €148 weekday or €130 weekend + 7% VAT

Meals: Breakfast included, Lunch/Dinner €32 including wine. The
restaurant is closed Sundays.

Getting there: From the airport head towards Málaga centre. Pass El
Corte Inglés and continue along the La Alameda. Turn left into Calle
Larios (at the statue of Marqués) and the hotel is on the left. Staff
will help with cases and parking. Or, easier still, park in the Plaza de
la Marina and take a taxi to the hotel.

Management: Pilar Quesada

It's amazing to think how many tourists fly into Málaga airport every year and how few actually visit this fascinating city. But the opening of the Picassao Museum will soon be pulling in the crowds. If you want a comfortable, safe stay right at the heart of its beautiful old centre, then book a room at the Larios. It is rather different in flavour to most of the other places included within the pages of this guide— it's a hotel that caters predominantly to business clientele and comes with the corresponding corporate features such as taped music, mini-bars, safes, satellite TVs, room service (and laundry) and uniformed reception staff. But – hey – we can all enjoy a bit of comfort and the rooms have double-glazing, the beds are top-notch and the rooftop bar is a brilliant place for an *apéritif* with a great view out to the floodlit Cathedral. All this business-class focus means that the price drops right down at the weekends, the obvious time to plan your visit. Here's a tip to enhance your stay—have a cocktail on the roof, then head out to the Antigua Casa de la Guardía for sherry and seafood.

To see and do: Málaga's old centre and the Picasso Museum, beaches and watersports, Los Montes de Málaga Natural Park

HOTEL CORTIJO LA REINA

MAP: 4

Ctra Colmenar km 548.5
29013 Málaga

Tel: 951 014000 **Fax:** 951 014049

e-mail: info@hotelcortijolareina.com

Web Page: www.hotelcortijolareina.com

Closed: Never

Bedrooms: 4 standard Doubles, 6 superior Doubles,
1 Junior Suite, 2 Houses and 1 wooden Cabin

Price: Standard Double €120-150, Superior Double €150-188,
Junior Suite €180-225, House €120-150,
Log Cabin €120-150 + 7% VAT

Meals: Breakfast included, Lunch/Dinner €30 including wine

Getting there: From Málaga take the N-340 towards Motril. Exit for
Limonar (km 244), go under the motorway then head back towards
Málaga. Exit for Ciudad Jardín, go under tunnel, then take the first left.
At the roundabout by 'Lidl' left again. At the next junction go left and
follow a winding road for 12km. The hotel is signposted to the right.

Management: Germán Gémar

An amazing road cuts north through the mountains from Málaga, twisting and looping its way to the heart of the Montes de Málaga Natural Park. The Cortijo de la Reina's private estate accounts for some 150 hectares of this protected area and, thanks to its 800 metre elevation, grabs an incredible view down to the coast. Arriving here, the line of cypress trees and the enormous pines that stand sentinel to the hotel are evocative of Tuscany or Provence. The decoration of the hotel, outside and in, is different to what you come to expect in a classic *cortijo*. Snazzy curtain fabrics and bright colour washes, rich burgundy rugs and damask sofas, masses of lamps and original oils work together to create a mood of elegant well-being. Music is piped through to all the public spaces (Viennese waltzes the day I visited). The hotel caters for both business people and tourists. The place really scores highly in its bedrooms which are sumptuously decorated and well worth the higher-than-usual price tag. Cortijo de la Reina's food, too, is fantastic thanks to a first class *jefe de cocina*; 'traditional food with gourmet touches' in the words of Germán.

To see and do: the Natural Park of Montes de Málaga, the old centre of Málaga and the Picasso museum, Antequera and the Torcal park

HOSPEDERÍA RETAMAR

MAP: 4

Partido Pujeo 30
Riogordo

Tel: 95 2031225 **Fax:** 95 2031209

Web Page: www.andalucia.com

Closed: Never

Bedrooms: 11 Doubles (some with a second single bed)

Price: Double €78-81 including VAT

Meals: Breakfast €6, Lunch/Dinner approx. €20 including wine

Getting there: From Málaga take the N-331 northwards then exit for Colmenar on the A-355. Bypass Colmenar and after 9km, exit for Riogordo and then follow the signs north to Retamar along 3km of track, soon to be tarmacked.

Management: José Sánchez Poderera

What is so wonderful about hotel-hopping in Andalusia is not just the places themselves but also the journey there. The wild beauty of the interior of this part of Spain never fails to move you. Cutting up the long track that leads up from Ríogordo to Retamar you find yourself in a magnificent stretch of wild, limestone mountains, softened occasionally by the olive and almond groves and a sprinkling of isolated farmsteads. The day I first came face to face with Retamar's beguiling palm-graced façade, a Shetland pony ambled across to greet me. This is one of the highest farms in La Axarquía and its hillside perch catches the breezes that blow up off the Mediterranean. It also explains the exceptionally mild climate of the area. Retamar's bedrooms have every modern convenience (TV, phones and air-conditioning) but what makes the place really special is the fantastic regional cooking. Mention should be made of the aubergines with honey, the snails (when in season) and fantastic cuts of meat served up sizzling on volcanic stones.

To see and do: walking in La Axarquía, day trip to Granada, visits to Antequera and El Torcal Natural Park

FINCA EL CERRILLO

MAP: 4

29755 Canillas de Albaida

Tel: 95 2030444 **Fax:** 95 2030444

e-mail: info@hotelfinca.com

Web Page: www.hotelfinca.com

Closed: Never

Bedrooms: 8 rooms and 1 Apartment sleeping up to 4

Price: Double/Twin €90, Apartment €120 including breakfast and VAT

Meals: Lunch €7, Dinner (available three times weekly) €24

Getting there: From Málaga go towards Motril on the N-340. Pass Exit 272 for Vélez-Málaga then take the next exit for Algarrobo/ Caleta. Head inland past Sayalonga then turn left to Archez. Here turn left towards Sedella/Salares. Cross a bridge, go up a hill then turn right at sign 'Fogarate'. El Cerrillo is on the right before you reach Canillas, where the tarmac surface becomes concreted.

Management: Sue & Gordon Kind

Canillas de Albaida is one of the prettiest of the villages of La Axarquía. Narrow streets wind up to its lovely hilltop chapel and the lush, subtropical valley that cuts north from here into the Tejeda Sierra is an absolute 'must-walk'. The hillsides around the village are peppered with small-holdings and one of the very loveliest of them, El Cerrillo, an ancient olive mill, has recently been converted into a wonderful small inn by its young English owners. Its position is stunning. There are massive views down towards the sea and a wonderful mature garden whose botanical highlights are its palms and an ancient carob. El Cerrillo has already made a name amongst the walking community but this is great place to chill out, too. There are stacks of books in the library, a massive beamed lounge and hidden corners of the garden where you can lounge your day away. The food is excellent—if you're feeling sociable it can be served at one large table. The bedrooms are simply fabulous, with the very swishest of bathrooms. Be sure to book at least two nights.

To see and do: walking in the Sierra de Tejeda y Almijara, Competa and Nerja

HOTEL RURAL LOS CARACOLES

MAP: 4

Ctra Frigiliana-Torrox km 4.7
Apartado de Correos 102
29788 Frigiliana

Tel: 95 2030680 or 95 2030609 **Fax:** 95 2030680

e-mail: hotelloscaracoles@ari.es

Web Page: www.hotelloscaracoles.com

Closed: Never

Bedrooms: 6 Double Snails (*caracoles*) and 6 Twins

Price: Twin €54-72, Caracol ('snail') €72-102 + 7% VAT

Meals: Breakfast €4.8, Lunch/Dinner €21-25 including wine. The restaurant is closed Mondays.

Getting there: From Málaga take the N-340 towards Motril then exit for Frigiliana/Nerja. Take the MA-105 to Frigiliana and here go round the bottom of the village, following signs for Torrox. Los Caracoles is 4.5km from Frigiliana, on the right.

Management: Julio Martín

When did you last sleep in...a snail (*caracol*)? This small hotel is
without question one of the most unusual places to stay in Andalusia.
The position is simply incredible—high above the quiet road which
cuts through the foothills of La Axarquía between Torrox and
Frigiliana and with the most exhilarating of views out across vine-
covered hillsides to Frigiliana and the sea. The extraordinary organic
architecture with its sinuous forms and extensive use of mosaic is
reminiscent of Gaudí's creations in the Catalan capital, while the
earthy colours evoke those of the Maghreb. And it all works
incredibly well. Pay the extra and book one of the 'snails' which has
been sculpted into the hillside so as to guarantee maximum
privacy and the best of views from its own private terrace. The
architecture of the restaurant is in the same vein and you'll be treated
to a culinary as well as an artistic/architectural feast. House
specialities include kid, ostrich with walnut sauce, suckling pig and
brochette of boar. And there's an interesting vegetarian menu
enhanced by the spicy flavours of North Africa.

To see and do: walking, beaches of the Cerro Gordo Natural Park,
visits to Frigiliana, Cómpeta and villages of La Axarquía

LA POSADA MORISCA

MAP: 4

Loma de la Cruz s/n
Ctra de montaña Frigiliana-Torrox
Frigiliana

Tel: 95 2534151 **Fax:** 95 2534339

e-mail: info@laposadamorisca.com

Web Page: www.laposadamorisca.com

Closed: 7 - 31 January

Bedrooms: 2 Doubles, 8 Twins and 2 Suites

Price: Double/Suite €80-125 including brekafast + 7% VAT

Meals: Breakfast included, Dinner €30 including wine

Getting there: From Málaga take the N-340 towards Motril then exit at km 292 for Frigiliana/Nerja. Then take the MA-105 to Frigiliana and here go round the bottom of the village, following signs for Torrox. 1.5km from Frigiliana, turn left at a sign for the hotel. Go down a steep track and then bear left to the Posada.

Management: Sara Navas Sánchez

La Posada Morisca is just a few kilometres from Frigiliana, terraced in amongst groves of avocado and mango in one of the most fertile parts of Andalusia's coastal fringe. You couldn't hope to meet with friendlier, kinder hosts than Sara and husband José Luis. The bedrooms that they worked long and hard to create are some of the nicest I've come across—a beautiful mix of rustic Spain (terracotta tiles, latticed wardrobes, wood-burning stoves, handmade tiles from Vélez) with a designer's eye for colour and fabrics. No two rooms are the same and all have panoramic views out to the Mediterranean. The decoration of the restaurant is just as aesthetically appealing— wafer brick, more terracotta and a bright, ceramic-tiled bar contrasted by floral curtains and soothing, creamy-coloured walls. The cooking is (to quote Sara) 'Mediterranean and innovative' with a fair portion of ingredients grown on the terraced slopes surrounding the farm. There are also some wonderful waymarked walks which pass close to the house, the most memorable of them being the Liman trail which cuts through the spectacular swathe of mountains to the south of Frigiliana, all the way to the coast.

To see and do: the caves at Nerja, Frigiliana, Cómpeta and villages of La Axarquía, beaches and *caletas* (coves) close to Maro

HOTEL PARAÍSO DEL MAR

MAP: 4

Calle Prolongación de Carabeo 22
29780 Nerja

Tel: 95 2521621 **Fax:** 95 2522309

e-mail: info@hispanica-colint.es

Web Page: www.hotelparaisodelmar.com

Closed: Mid November - mid December

Bedrooms: 2 Singles, 4 'normal' Double/Twins, 3 Double/Twins
with jacuzzi/sea views and 3 Suites

Price: Single €50-125, Double/Twin €60-104, Double with jacuzzi
€82-116, Suite €102-140 + 7% VAT

Meals: Breakfast included, no Lunch/Dinner available, but lots of
local and international restaurants within an easy walk of hotel

Getting there: Round Málaga on the N-340 towards Almería then
exit for Nerja. Here follow the signs for the Parador. Hotel Paraíso
del Mar is just a few metres away at the edge of the Balcón de
Europa.

Management: Enrique Caro Bernal

You'll probably remember two things about Hotel El Paraiso del Mar. One will be the stunning location high above Nerja's long sweep of golden sand. The other will be meeting Enrique Caro Bernal. He is one of a rare breed of hoteliers who, even at the end of the season, is able to greet you with the same warmth and enthusiasm as he would his very first guest. Nowadays visitors will book their holidays a year in advance, yet this is not a man to rest on his laurels. Not a year passes without some part of his small hotel being refurbished or refurnished. The hotel has gradually been built up round what was once the private villa of an English doctor. Later additions have been built in such a way that you'd have difficulty saying where the original building ends and the new one begins. Several bedrooms and suites have balconies and/or terraces that look out across the cliff-side, terraced gardens to the beach which can be reached by a steep path that drops down from the hotel. Without doubt this is one of the coast's friendliest small hotels.

To see and do: the Nerja caves, el Balcón de Europa, Frigiliana

HOTEL ROMANTICO CASA MARO

MAP: 4

Calle del Carmen 2
29787 Maro

Tel: 95 2529552 or 95 2529690 or 627 958456 **Fax:** 95 2529552

e-mail: hotelcasamaro@teleline.es

Web Page: www.guideofnerja.com

Closed: Never

Bedrooms: 2 Singles, 2 Doubles and 6 Studios with own kitchen

Price: Single €45, Small Double €45, Studios €79 including VAT

Meals: Breakfast €7-12, Lunch/Dinner €25-50 including wine in gourmet bistro

Getting there: From Málaga take the N-340 towards Motril then exit for Nerja. Go through Nerja to Maro and there take the first right as you enter the village. You'll see the Casa Maro on the left.

Management: Paul Ott

As you'd expect given its full name, Hotel Romantico Casa Maro could be just the place for a romantic break. Maro is a tiny cluster of houses above one of the nicest coves and beaches on this part of the coast, a short drive from Nerja's famous *Balcón de Europa* and cave. This sleepy hamlet had a brief moment of glory when a factory was built to extract sugar but sank back into obscurity once it closed. You'll have no problem spotting the salmon and peppermint-green walls of Casa Maro which had me thinking of villas along the Côte d'Azur. The place would make a great film-set for a Graham Greene novel—the vintage car, the three macaws that officiate over a palm-shaded terrace, potted orchids and aspidistra and views out across groves of avocado and custard-fruit to the sea. The hotel is known (by its mostly German-speaking devotees) for its gourmet food. Fresh fish is nearly always on offer as well as plenty of fresh vegetables and interesting sauces. Maro's bedrooms are in a more simple vein. Those on the ground-floors are small whilst those on the first floor are lighter and more spacious. The accent is on simple comfort—teamaker and fridge are welcome extras, wth the best rooms looking out to the sea.

To see and do: the Nerja caves, the beaches of Maro, the villages of La Axarquía

CÓRDOBA
PROVINCE

HOTELS 094 TO 099

A Flowered Patio of Córdoba

HOSPEDERIA DE SAN FRANCISCO

MAP: 3

Avenida Pío XII 35
14700 Palma del Río

Tel: 957 710183 **Fax:** 957 645146

e-mail: hospederia@casasypalacios.com

Web Page: www.casasypalacios.com

Closed: Never

Bedrooms: 14 Doubles and 23 Twins

Price: Double/Twin €84-97 + 7% VAT

Meals: Breakfast included, Lunch/Dinner €25 excluding wine

Getting there: From Córdoba take the N-IV towards Sevilla. Exit just before Écija on A-453 to Palma del Río then follow the signs to the hotel.

Management: Jesús Rojas

The year 1492 was, as we all know, quite a year for Spain. America was discovered as Columbus sailed west to get east and those pesky Moors were finally sent packing. It was also the year that the 7th Lord of Palma left orders in his Last Testament that a Franciscan monastery should be built. His will was carried out and the monastery he funded served as a retreat for the Brothers until 1985 when it was given a new destiny as one of Andalusia's most charismatic small hotels. The bedrooms, in what were the monk's cells, are wrapped around a series of linked cloisters and patios where ochre, salmon and earth-brown pigments highlight columns and arches in a wonderful symphony of form and colour. The rooms are simply fabulous. Their dark wooden furniture, religious prints and original tiled floors hark back to times past, whilst their sparkling bathrooms talk of a different age. There's a Basque chef officiating over culinary matters but if you fancy something less elaborate, start your evening with a drink in the hotel's bar then head for the centre of town where there are a number of friendly *tapas* bars.

To see and do: the Sierra de Hornachuelos Natural Park, the old town of Palma del Río, Córdoba and Sevilla

HOTEL ALBUCASIS

MAP: 3

Buen Pastor 11
14003 Córdoba

Tel: 957 478625 **Fax:** 957 478625

Closed: 6 January - 7 February

Bedrooms: 6 Singles and 9 Doubles

Price: Single €45, Double €72 including VAT

Meals: Breakfast €5, no Lunch/Dinner available, but a huge choice of restaurants and *tapas* bars within walking distance

Getting there: Follow signs to Plaza de las Tendillas then take streets Jesús María, Ángel de Saavedra, Blanco Belmonte, Conde y Luque and finally Buen Pastor to the hotel which will be on your right. But it's much easier to park in any city centre car park and take a taxi to the hotel.

Management: Alfonso Sales Camacho

Staying somewhere in Córdoba's Jewish quarter has to be first choice if you visit the city, not least because its incredibly narrow streets (laid out with donkeys rather than cars in mind) guarantee a minimum of traffic nuisance. My personal favourite *judería* (Jewish quarter) address is Hotel Albucasis. It is quiet, clean, comfortable, just metres from the synagogue and only a five minute stroll from the Mezquita. You are also just out of the touristy-tack shadow, in a part of town where shopkeepers receive you with a smile. The Spanish and Andalusian flags hanging over the entrance will help you spot the hotel. Its portal of dressed stone leads to a pleasant inner courtyard where white, rather rococo wrought-iron garden furniture feels a bit out of synch with the subdued mood of the simple lounge-cum-breakfast room with high French windows that capture a maximum amount of light. It is absolutely spotless and in one corner there's a small bar where you can always get a drink. Bedrooms are simple affairs with marble floors and louvre-doored wardrobes: the nicest is no. 33 which looks out over the rooftops of this enchanting part of Córdoba.

To see and do: the Mezquita and the Jewish quarter, palace complex of Medina Azahara, walking in the Sierra Morena

HOTEL AMISTAD

MAP: 3

Plaza de Maimónides 3
14004 Córdoba

Tel: 957 420335 **Fax:** 957 420365

e-mail: nhamistadcordoba@nh-hotels.com

Web Page: www.nh-hotels.com

Closed: Never

Bedrooms: 2 Singles, 18 Doubles and 64 Twins

Price: Double/Twin €146 + VAT

Meals: Breakfast €14, Lunch/Dinner €40-45 including wine

Getting there: Arriving from the south, cross the river and then follow the signs for Amistad (with P = Parking sign). The hotel car park is just beyond the Almudaina restaurant (ignore the No Entry sign).

Management: Francisco Javier Muñoz Valadez

NH Amistad manages to break the mould of the standard "chain" hotel. Although it is much larger than other hotels in this book, thanks to the friendliness of its staff and the unusual architecture of the place (it embraces a part of the city walls and some rooms are in a separate annex), it feels both intimate and welcoming. It is also brilliantly central. From here, through the labyrinth of alleyways in the Jewish quarter, you can walk to the Mezquita in just five minutes. Arriving in its very swish reception area (marble is used as a cooling element throughout the hotel) you at first scc little sign of the two 18th century mansions that were renovated to create the hotel. Things begin to feel more authentic in the beautiful pebbled inner patio where a fountain and wafer-bricked arches hark back to another age. All bedrooms (the nicest are Nos. 201-208) have four-star fittings, snazzy bathrooms, marbled or parquet floors and every conceivable modern convenience. The buffet breakfast is excellent, too, but I'd skip supper and instead head out to eat in one of the more intimate restaurants of the old Jewish quarter.

To see and do: the Mezquita and the Jewish quarter, palace complex of Medina Azahara, walking in the Sierra Morena

HOSTAL SENECA

MAP: 3

Conde y Luque 7
14003 Córdoba

Tel: 957 473234 **Fax:** 957 473234

Closed: Closed over Christmas period for about 1 month

Bedrooms: 1 Single, 4 doubles and 7 Twins, some sharing bathrooms

Price: Single €14-26, Double/Twin with bathroom €33-36, Double/Twin sharing bathroom €26-29 including VAT

Meals: Breakfast included, no Lunch/Dinner available, but a huge choice of restaurants and *tapas* bars within walking distance

Getting there: Hostal Seneca is in a narrow street just to the north of the Mezquita. Park anywhere in the centre and take a taxi to the hotel—it is difficult to negotiate the very narrow streets of the Jewish quarter.

Management: Janine Peignier & María del Pilar Romero

If you're travelling on a budget, Hostal Seneca could be a brilliant choice. It certainly isn't grand and if you're one to hanker after bathrobes, satellite TV and minibars then this place won't be for you. This is a typical rambling *Córdoban* townhouse with a plant-filled pebbled patio whose striped arches and columns are evocative of those of the Mezquita which is less than 100 yards from the Seneca. This is a very old house. There was a dwelling here during the Moorish period and there's evidence, too, that parts of it date back to Roman times. The house's last big reform was in 1860 and many of the floor tiles, stucco mouldings and the wonderful geometric tiles are from that period. You may not meet with the owners but the friendly, gregarious manager Juan takes good care of his guests, officiating in the tiny wood and tile clad breakfast room-cum-bar. The simple bedrooms follow the twists and turns of the house's original floor plan and vary in size and configuration. The Seneca gets a mention in all the guides, so you'll need to book ahead.

To see and do: the Mezquita and the Jewish quarter, the palace complex of Medina Azahara, walking in the Sierra Morena

HOTEL ZUHAYRA

MAP: 4

Calle Mirador 10
14870 Zuheros

Tel: 957 694693 or 957 694694 **Fax:** 957 694702

e-mail: hotelzuhayra@zuheros.com

Web Page: www.zuheros.com

Closed: Never

Bedrooms: 4 Doubles and 14 Twins

Price: Double/Twin €43-55 + 7% VAT

Meals: Breakfast included, Lunch/Dinner €11-20 excluding wine

Getting there: From Málaga head north towards Córdoba on the N-331 to Lucena. As you leave the town turn right at signs for Cabra. Here go towards Doña Mencía before turning right to Zuheros. Leave your car in the car park by the castle. The hotel is on the right as you go down Calle Mirador.

Management: José & Juan Carlos Ábalos Guerrero

It's puzzling to think why Zuheros isn't better known. It is the most spectacular of villages with whitewashed houses clinging to an outcrop of limestone rock and topped by a high castle. Make the detour and stay at Hotel Zuhayra. From the outside it's a rather unexciting edifice but thanks to its prominent location, all of its bedrooms look out across the town. They are sparklingly clean with simple pine furniture and the fabrics of bedspreads and curtains have all just been changed. I love their uncluttered feel and they are very well equipped given their price. On the ground floor there's a large, rather dark bar area. Much nicer in feel is the cosy first floor restaurant where the menu looks to traditional, Andalusian country cuisine. Specialities include wonderful *salmorejo* (a thick gazpacho), *remojón* (made with hake and oranges), aubergines cooked with honey and some interesting salad variations—a rare thing in Andalusia. The two brothers who run the hotel are exceptionally friendly and there are wonderful walks leading out from the village.

To see and do: walking in the Subbética Natural Park, La Cueva de los Murcielagos (the cave of the bats), the castle and museum of Zuheros

POSADA REAL

MAP: 4

Calle Real 14
14800 Priego de Córdoba

Tel: 957 541910 **Fax:** 957 540993

e-mail: posadar@arrakis.es

Web Page: www.laposadareal.com

Closed: Never

Bedrooms: 2 Twins with own bathroom, 1 Twin and 1 Double sharing bathroom and 1 Apartment for 4

Price: Double/Twin €45, Apartment for 4 €75 including VAT

Meals: Breakfast included (unless in apartment), no Lunch/Dinner available. Excellent tapas bars and restaurants are very close to the Posada.

Getting there: Go north from Málaga to Lucena on the N-331. Just past Lucena take the A-336 via Cabra to Priego. Here follow the signs, *centro ciudad* then, *casco antiguo/histórico*. Park your car in the Plaza del Castillo (locals call it the 'Plaza del Llano'). Calle Real leads off this square.

Management: Juan López Calvo

Wandering the narrow streets of Priego de Córdoba's old centre feels like returning to another age. In this plexus of narrow alleyways there is no passing traffic to shatter that illusion. And at the heart of what the locals call the *villa* (town), the tiny Posada Real must be first choice if you stay a night here. When Juan López Calvo restored this old house he wanted to make things as authentically *andaluz* as possible. The fruit of his labour is a place to stay that feels far more like a home than a hotel. There are just four bedrooms (plus a flat up under the eaves), each with its own balcony. They have been beautifully decorated by Juan and his family with antiques, old engravings and rich fabrics. Bathrooms have hand-painted tiles and 'repro' taps. In the warmer months you breakfast in a quiet vine-covered patio where you are treated to freshly squeezed orange juice, local goat's cheese and quince jelly. Just metres away in the adjacent *plaza* is the excellent Abravadero restaurant. Don't consider leaving town without visiting the extraordinary Fuente del Rey, another of Andalusia's unsung treasures.

To see and do: the Route of the Baroque of Córdoba including the Fuente del Rey, walking in Subbética Park, the Roman ruins of Almedinilla

GRANADA PROVINCE

HOTELS 100 TO 115

A terraced valley in the Alpujarras

HOTEL LA BOBADILLA

MAP: 4

Apartado de Correos 144
18300 Loja

Tel: 958 321861 **Fax:** 958 321810

e-mail: info@la-bobadilla.com

Web Page: www.la-bobadilla.com

Closed: Never

Bedrooms: 2 Singles, 12 Doubles, 11 Twins,
28 Junior Suites and 9 Suites

Price: Single €181-226, Double/Twin €264-303,
Junior Suite €342-391, Suite €461-940

Meals: Breakfast included, Lunch/Dinner €44 excluding wine

Getting there: From Málaga take the N-331 then the A-359 towards
Granada. Take Exit 1 for Salinas then follow the signs for Villanueva
de Tapia. The hotel is signposted to the right of the road.

Management: Mariano Verdejo Vendrell

The Bobadilla probably offers the most luxurious, most exotic hotel experience in Andalusia—an amazing cocktail of *Arabian Nights* fantasy with a liberal dash of Hollywood. A 1000 acre estate of holm-oak forest, olive groves and almond groves protect the hotel from the outside world. The place is known by tour operators the world over and especially by the Japanese who are crazy to get married here. They come for the amazing rooms and suites, the excellent gourmet cuisine (choose between one of three restaurants) and the enormous range of activities on offer. There are Turkish baths, saunas, jacuzzis, an indoor pool, a gym, archery, riding and tennis. You can shoot, fly over the farm in a light aircraft or a hot air balloon, canoe or kayak, tour the grounds on foot or by 4 wheel drive. You can have a facial or be pampered by a masseur. The King of Spain has stayed, Placido Domingo too and, wow! - Tom Cruise and Brad Pitt have slept here as well. So get the bank to up your credit card limit and head for Xanadu, right here in the hills of Andalusia.

To see and do: Antequera and the Torcal Natural Park, Archidona, Granada and the Alhambra

PALACIO DE SANTA INES

MAP: 5

Cuesta de Santa Inés 9, Barrio del Albaicín
18010 Granada

Tel: 958 222362 **Fax:** 958 222465

e-mail: sinespal@teleline.es

Web Page: www.palaciodesantines.com

Closed: Never

Bedrooms: 4 standard Double/Twins, 26 larger Double/Twins,
3 Suites and the Alhambra Suite

Price: Standard Double/Twin €100, Larger Double/Twin €120-150,
Suite €150, Alhambra Suite €225 + 7% VAT

Meals: Breakfast €8, no Lunch/Dinner available. but a huge choice
of restaurants and *tapas* bars within walking distance

Getting there: Follow the signs for the centre and then to Plaza
Nueva. Here take the narrow Carrera del Darro and by the first
bridge stop and walk up Cuesta de Santa Inés to the hotel. One of
their staff will help you park. But it is much easier to park in any
central car park and then take a taxi to the hotel.

Management: Nicolás Garrido

The best views of the Alhambra are to be had from the Albaicín Hill on the opposite bank of the River Darro. Don't miss climbing up to the San Nicolás mirador. A dozen years ago this was a run-down part of town but it is fast becoming the place to live. Just metres from the lively *tapas* bars lining the course of the river, the Palacio de Santa Inés is one of the city's most attractive small hotels. Like so many of Andalusia's houses, the façade of this 16th century mansion gives little away. But things step up a beat when you pass into the wonderful balustraded, marble-columned patio. The hotel's most memorable features are its Renaissance murals, attributed to a pupil of Raphael, and the intricate *mudéjar* (post-conquest Moorish style architecture) woodwork of some of its ceilings, the most remarkable being that of the Alhambra Suite. The bedrooms (several more are being added as we go to press) stylishly marry antiques, modern art and richly coloured *kilims*. There are always cut flowers to greet you. Some of the rooms look straight out to the Alhambra.

To see and do: the Alhambra of course, the Carthusian monastery of La Cartuja, the Albaicín area

HOSTAL SUECIA

MAP: 5

Calle Molinos, Huerta de los Angeles 8
18009 Granada

Tel: 958 225044 or 958 227781 **Fax:** 958 225044

Closed: Never

Bedrooms: 2 Doubles and 7 Twins with own bathrooms,
1 Double and 2 Twins sharing two bathrooms

Price: Double/Twin with bathrom €48-51,
Double/Twin sharing bathroom €40 including VAT

Meals: Breakfast €4.50, no Lunch/Dinner available, but a huge
choice of restaurants and *tapas* bars a short walk away in Campo del
Príncipe

Getting there: Round Granada on the ringroad, following signs for
the Alhambra. Go uphill towards the Alhambra following the signs to
the Alhambra Palace Hotel. Here go left down Antequerela Baja and
take the next sharp right to Campo del Príncipe. Cross the square left
into Calle Molinos, then turn left again under the arch to the Suecia.

Management: Mari-Carmen Cerdán Mejías

Don't expect the moon if you come and stay at the Suecia. But if you
are looking for a quiet, friendly and unassuming place to stay close
to the Alhambra that won't cost an arm or a leg, then you're bound to
enjoy this modest *hostal*. The position is wonderful, right at the end
of a quiet *cul-de-sac* and just a five minute stroll from the Campo del
Príncipe, a lively square which has dozens of bars and restaurants.
The house's façade strikes a merry note with balconied windows
picked out by broad bands of ochre and its small front garden awash
in greenery. Can you really be in a city centre? One of the hotel's
long-serving staff greets you and hands over your key. The Suecia's
bedrooms are on the first and second floor and are simply decorated
with wooden furniture, sugary prints and light green curtains and
bedspreads. Nothing fancy but perfectly adequate. Breakfasts are
served in the small, second floor dining room that looks out onto a
roof top terrace. From here there are wonderful views of the
Alhambra hill, without doubt the hotel's most special feature.

To see and do: the Alhambra of course, the Carthusian monastery of
La Cartuja, the Albaicín area

HOTEL CARMEN DE SANTA INÉS

MAP: 5

Placeta de Porras 7
San Juan de los Reyes
18010 Granada

Tel: 958 226380 or 958 224511 **Fax:** 958 224404

e-mail: sinescar@teleline.es

Web Page: www.carmensantaines.com

Closed: Never

Bedrooms: 7 Doubles, 2 Twin, 1 Suite

Price: Double €90-120, Twin €100-120, Suite €195 + 7% VAT

Meals: Breakfast €8, no Lunch/Dinner available, but a huge choice of restaurants and *tapas* bars within walking distance

Getting there: Don't try driving here! It is best to park in Parking San Agustín (or any other city centre car park) and take a taxi to the hotel. The narrow streets of the Albaicín are a nightmare to negotiate.

Management: Nicolás Garrido

Granada's *carmens* are amongst Andalusia's most attractive architectural creations. The term *carmen* is used to describe a townhouse with a walled garden. They nearly always have an intimate, hidden-world feel about them and many of those on Granada's Albaicín hill are from Moorish times. After an extensive reform in the 17th century, the Carmen de Santa Inés has a rather more grand air than most. The building's soul is its tiny patio-courtyard where the song of a simple marble fountain is the first sound to greet you when you come in from the Albaicín's narrow streets. A heavy wooden door leads out to the garden where another fountain echoes the water music and where the view of the Alhambra is a heady enticement to sit and while away an afternoon. Nicolás Garrido has worked wonders with the Carmen's decoration which, like the nearby Palacio de Santa Inés, is an attractive *potpourri* of antiques, modern art and warm colour washes. Suites are worth the extra euros (the normal doubles are rather small) and the Mirador is the best room with its view across to the Alhambra.

To see and do: the Alhambra of course, the Carthusian monastery of La Cartuja, the Albaicín area

HOTEL AMERICA

MAP: 5

Real de La Alhambra 53
18009 Granada

Tel: 958 227471 **Fax:** 958 227470

e-mail: reservas@hotelamericagranada.com

Web Page: www.hotelamericagranada.com

Closed: Never

Bedrooms: 4 Singles, 6 Doubles and 5 Twins

Price: Single €65, Double/Twin €100 including VAT

Meals: Breakfast €7, simple Lunches €20 excluding wine.
The restaurant is closed at weekends.

Getting there: Round Granada following signs for the Alhambra on
the 'Ronda Sur' ringroad. Go up the hill towards the Alhambra then
follow signs to the hotel, making sure to keep to the left so as not to
enter car parks. Leave baggage at the hotel and then leave your car in
one of the Alhambra car parks.

Management: Maribel Alconchel

For years and years Hotel America has been one of the very best places to stay in Granada. There's only one problem. Unless you book weeks ahead, chances are that it will be full. The reason for its popularity is not only that it is an immensely attractive hotel just metres from the Alhambra, but also because of the good, old-fashioned hospitality of the Alonchel family. Three generations of them have managed the America since it opened it doors in 1936. Previous to that it had been the summer residence of a well-to-do Duchess. Guests invariably gravitate towards a plant-filled courtyard which doubles as the hotel's restaurant. Here sparrows hop between ceramic-topped tables and a Virginia creeper and rambling ivy help keep the sun at bay. It can get busy at lunchtime so it is best enjoyed later in the day when the coach parties are heading back down the hill. I would try to book a bedroom on the top floor (Nos. 212 or 214) which have recently been completely redecorated in a warm ochre tones and which feel as welcoming as the rest of the hotel.

To see and do: the Alhambra of course, the Carthusian monastery of La Cartuja, the Albaicín area

HOTEL CASA MORISCA

MAP: 5

Cuesta de la Victoria 9
18010 Granada

Tel: 958 221100 **Fax:** 958 215796

e-mail: info@hotelcasamorisca.com

Web Page: www.hotelcasamorisca.com

Closed: Never

Bedrooms: 2 Singles, 5 Doubles, 9 Twins and 1 Suite

Price: Single €89-112, Double/Twin €111-140,
Suite €190 + 7% VAT

Meals: Breakfast €9, no Lunch/Dinner available, but a huge choice
of restaurants and *tapas* bars within walking distance

Getting there: From the Plaza Nueva follow the Acera del Darro
almost to the end (the Alhambra will be to your right) and the Cuesta
de La Victoria is last-but-one turning to the left. Or, more simply,
park anywhere in the centre and take a taxi to hotel.

Management: María Jesús Candenas & Carlos Sánchez

The Casa Morisca is amongst a number of Albaicín mansion houses which have been transformed into small hotels. This is a very old house. The owners have documents tracing its origins back to the end of the 15th century. As its name suggests, the architecture of the house is that beloved of the Moors, a style that continued to be prevalent long after their expulsion. Here are wafer-brick columns, delicate keyhole arches, polychromatic tiles with Arabic calligraphy and the most amazing of *mudéjar* (post conquest Moorish syle of architecture) wooden ceilings. This is the perfect place to stay to prolong that Alhambra moment, and from many of the fourteen bedrooms you look straight out to the Comares tower. All rooms have been magnificently decorated. There are intricate Alhambra-style mouldings, bright *kilims*, pastel colours and fabulous bath-rooms. The lighting is subtle, the beds superb and the place is surprisingly quiet given the city centre location. You breakfast in a barrel-vaulted dining room, your meal accompanied by the musical gurgling of the courtyard fountain.

To see and do: the Alhambra of course, the Albaicín area and the Carrera del Darro (great *tapas* bars)

CASA DEL CAPITEL NAZARÍ

MAP: 5

Cuesta Aceituneros, 6
Albayzín-Plaza Nueva
18010 Granada

Tel: 958 215260 **Fax:** 958 215806

e-mail: info@hotelcasacapitel.com

Web Page: www.hotelcasacapitel.com

Closed: Never

Bedrooms: 10 Doubles and 7 Twins

Price: Double/Twin €85 + 7% VAT

Meals: Breakfast €8

Getting there: Best to park in the Aparcamiento Plaza Puerta Real
in the centre of Granada. Take a taxi from the rank immediately
outside and the hotel will refund the cost.

Management: Mari-Luz Cerón

The Darro gorge cuts a deep cleft through Granada's old centre.
From its northern bank the narrow streets of the Albaicín quarter cut
anarchically upwards, a plexus of narrow alleyways with an architectural delight around every corner. Since being declared a Unesco
World Heritage site the area has seen huge changes, including the
opening of a number of small hotels. The Casa del Capitel is
amongst the best of them, and is excellent value given its location
and degree of comfort. The bedrooms are reached by way of a
columned and balconied courtyard. They are smallish but feel snug
rather than stifling and have warm colour washes, wooden ceilings,
retro taps, nice lamps and all the add-ons like air-conditioning, TVs,
telephones and mini-bars. The building is a fascinating *potpourri* of
architectural elements—a Renaissance *palacete* (grand townhouse)
with Roman columns, a Moorish *capitel* (hence the name) and
magnificent polychromatic *mudejar* geometric ceilings whose
restoration took more than three years. The nicest room is Number
22 which has a 16th century carved ceiling and a view of the
crenelated walls of the Alhambra. The staff are delightful, too.

To see and do: The Alhambra, the Cathedral and the Royal chapel,
exploring the narrow streets of the Albaicín

CASA DEL ALJARIFE

MAP: 5

Placeta de la Cruz Verde 2
18010 Granada

Tel: 958 222425 **Fax:** 958 222425

e-mail: most@wanadoo.es

Web Page: www.granadainfo.com/most

Closed: Never

Bedrooms: 1 Double, 2 Twins and 1 Suite for 4

Price: Double/Twin €89, Suite €89-168 + 7% VAT

Meals: Continental breakfast €5, Brunch including cold meats and cheeses €10

Getting there: Park in any city centre car park. The nearest is Aparcamiento San Agustín. Then take a taxi to the Plaza Nueva. Ring Christian, who will come down and guide you to the Casa del Aljarife.

Management: María del Carmen López García & Christian Most

The Albayzín district should always be your first choice when spending a night in Granada. Strung out along the Darro gorge there are masses of lively of bars and restaurants, the views across to the Alhambra are enchanting and its plexus of narrow alleyways speaks of a different age. Christian and María del Carmen had already bought and restored this grand 17th century house long before the area became the place to live in Granada. Like so many of the Albaicín's houses, the façade gives little away but once you pass through the heavy wooden doors you emerge into a huge cobbled courtyard where a deliciously rambling garden of laurel, jasmine, aspidistra and bougainvillea evoke passages from *Arabian Nights*. This is the place where you'll inevitably spend most of your time but the bedrooms too, are really comfortable—air-conditioned for the summer, centrally heated for the winter. A couple of rooms grab a view of the Alhambra. Christian is a cheery host and has thoughtfully compiled his own small listing of the town's best bars and restaurants and of the visiting times for Granada's most interesting monuments.

To see and do: the Albaicín, the Alhambra, the cathedral and the Carthusian monastery of La Cartuja

EL CORTIJO DEL PINO

MAP: 4

Fernán Nuñez 2, La Loma
18659 Albuñuelas

Tel: 958 776257 **Fax:** 958 776250

e-mail: cortijodelpino@eresmas.com

Web Page: www.cortijodelpino.official.es

Closed: Never

Bedrooms: 1 Single, 1 Double, 3 Twins or complete house rental (during summer & at Easter)

Price: Single €45, Double/Twin €75 or complete house rented for €1575 per week including VAT

Meals: Breakfast included, no meals Dinner €15 excluding wine

Getting there: Take the N-331 from Málaga to Granada, the NA-359, then the A-92. Just before Granada branch onto the A-323 towards Motril and take Exit 153 for Albuñuelas. As you arrive in the village, turn right by a bus stop. A steep road leads you up to El Cortijo del Pino.

Management: Antonia Ruano & James Connel

You can spot the massive Aleppo pine tree that towers above Cortijo del Pino from kilometres away. It's what gives the house its name. The tree stands guardian to the old farmhouse that this Anglo-Spanish couple have recently turned into one of Andalusia's most attractive small B&Bs. They run it in the very best tradition of *mi casa es tu casa* (my home is your home). James is an artist and sometimes gives courses at the house (details on request). There is plenty to inspire, whether you want to paint a still life or a landscape. Every corner of this house has been decorated and arranged with an artist's sensitivity, and the views out across the wooded valley to Albuñuelas are magnificent. You won't want for space in the bedrooms, which Antonia has skillfully decorated with family antiques, huge beds, beautiful tiles, hand-embroidered curtains and, of course, James' paintings. When I stayed at El Pino I awoke to the sound of birdsong and the chiming of church bells from across the valley. I also have wonderful memories of a delicious dinner in the very best of company.

To see and do: the Alhambra, the villages of La Alpujarra, the Costa Tropical

LA TARTANA

MAP: 4

Urbanización San Nicolás
18697 La Herradura

Tel: 958 640535 **Fax:** 958 640535

e-mail: reservations@hotellatartana.com

Web Page: www.hotellatartana.com

Closed: Never

Bedrooms: 4 Doubles and 2 Twins

Price: Double/Twin €55-79 + 7% VAT

Meals: Breakfast included, Dinner €15-25 excluding wine

Getting there: From Málaga, take the N-340 east towards Motril. Approximately 15 minutes past Nerja, pass the km 308 marker post and at the next traffic lights change direction and head back towards Málaga. Then take the first right into Urbanización San Nicolás. The hotel is the first building on the left.

Management: Penny Jarret, Barry Branham and Joachim Holter

La Tartana is one of this part of the coast's oldest guest houses and has recently seen a complete metamorphosis thanks to the combined *savoir-faire* of its new owners. The hotel is just back from the busy N-340 and although you can hear the traffic it hardly detracts from the place's high feel-good factor. The garden is wonderful—there are views out to the sparkling ocean. The bedrooms, all of which have been recently redecorated, look on to a balconied, central patio with a rambling creeper and a pretty sandstone fountain. What lifts the place into the 'special' category is the restaurant. If you want a change from the traditional *andaluz* food then Tartana's cuisine, which takes its lead from California and 'world food', will revive your appetite. Ingredients are always fresh, flavours inspired and the pastry truly exceptional. This would be a great choice for a first or a last night in Spain—you are an easy drive from the airport. There are also good beaches close by and Granada is an easy day trip from here. Penny, Barry and Joachím make each and every one of their guests feel special.

To see and do: beaches and water sports, hiking and Granada and the Sierra Nevada an easy drive away

HOTEL ALBERGUE DE MECINA

MAP: 6

Calle La Fuente s/n
18416 Mecina Fondales

Tel: 958 766241 or 958 766241 **Fax:** 958 766255

e-mail: victor@hoteldemecina.com

Web Page: www.ocioteca.com/hoteldemecina

Closed: Never

Bedrooms: 3 Doubles, 5 Triples and 13 Quadruples

Price: Double €60, Triple €75 and Quadruple €85 + 7% VAT

Meals: Breakfast €5.50, Lunch/Dinner €12-18 excluding wine

Getting there: From Granada take the new motorway south towards
Motril then exit on the C-333 through Lanjarón. As you reach
Órgiva take the road via Pampaneira towards Pitres. Turn right down
the hill to Mecina 1km before Pitres. The hotel is at the top of
the village.

Management: Victor M. Fernandez

More and more people are visiting the Alpujarras, especially at the weekends. Tourist shops now line the streets of places like Pampaneira and Trevélez. You'll escape the crowds at the Albergue de Mecina which is in one of the area's lesser known villages. The hotel has been open for several years but it is only since Victor Fernandez has been at the helm that the hotel has begun to make waves. Be sure to ask for one of the rooms at the rear of the building which has views out across the steep-sided *barranco* (gorge) of the River Trevélez. Most of them are massive and have been redecorated and refurnished with bright fabrics, dark wooden bedside tables and dressers and pictures with a floral theme. The hotel's best feature is its dining room which is decorated in a more rustic style than the bedrooms. Dark beams support a traditional dark slate roof, tables are prettily laid with pink cloths and cut flowers, and the food is excellent—all the typical dishes of the Alpujarras (like the hearty *plato alpujarreño*). Some of the ingredients come fresh from the Albergue's organic vegetable garden.

To see and do: walking, the Roman bridge in Fondales, the Buddhist monastery above Pampaneira

ALQUERÍA DE MORAYMA

MAP: 6

A-348 Cádiar-Torvizcón km 52
18440 Cádiar

Tel: 958 343221 or 958 343303 **Fax:** 958 343221

e-mail: alqueria@alqueriamorayma

Web Page: www.alqueriamorayma.com

Closed: Never

Bedrooms: 3 Doubles, 10 Twins and 5 Apartments

Price: Double/Twin €54-59, Apartment for 2 or 3 €63, Apartment for 4 €83-91 + 7% VAT

Meals: Breakfast €3, Lunch/Dinner €12-18 including wine

Getting there: From Granada take the N-323 south towards Motril then exit on the A-348 to Lanjarón. Here continue to Órgiva and Torvizcón towards Cádiar. The Alquería de Morayma is 2km before Cádiar, to the left of the road.

Management: Mariano Cruz Fajardo

The Alquería de Morayma lies just east of the deep *barranco* (gorge) that author Chris Stewart recently put on the map in his best-selling *Driving Over Lemons*. This is fantastic walking country and the long distance foot-path that winds its way across the Alpujarra passes just metres from Morayma. Mariano Cruz wanted to create something more than a place to sleep and eat at La Alquería. He wanted guests to actually immerse themselves in the traditional way of life of the area. So you can join in with the harvest and the milling of the farm's olives, you can help to make goat's cheese, bring in the grapes or even take part in the winter *matanza* (the slaughter and preparation of a pig). This is a place where you'd want to spend several nights. The rooms and houses recreate the feel of one of the region's villages —an organic, inter-linked whole that centres round the bar and restaurant. The rooms have been conceived as comfortable living spaces as well as an ethnographical testament to all that is local. The restaurant's menu, as you'd expect, offers the same time-tried recipes that you might find in any traditional Alpujarran home.

To see and do: walking and horse-riding, visit to a *secadero* where cured hams are prepared, and visits to the villages of the Alpujarra

HOTEL LA FRAGUA

MAP: 6

Calle San Antonio 4
18417 Trevélez

Tel: 958 858626 or 958 858512 **Fax:** 958 858614

e-mail: informacion@hotelafragua.com

Closed: Early January - early February

Bedrooms: 4 Singles, 4 Doubles, 6 Twins and
10 Doubles/Twins with terraces

Price: Single €25, Double/Twin €34,
Double/Twin with terrace €40 + 7% VAT

Meals: Breakfast €2.75, Lunch/Dinner €12-15 including wine

Getting there: From Granada take the new motorway south towards
Motril then exit on the C-333. Go through Lanjarón and just before
Órgiva turn left toTrevélez. Here go steeply uphill to the *barrio
medio* and park near to La Plaza de las Pulgas. La Fragua is next to
the *Ayuntamiento* (town hall).

Management: Antonio & Miguel Espinosa

Trevélez is one of the better-known villages in the Alpujarras, especially amongst the walking community. From here you can climb the Sierra Nevada's highest peak, the Mulhacén (you´ll be starting at a height of nearly 1500m!) and the GR-7 long-distance footpath loops past the village. La Fragua is one of the village's highest buildings; from its rooftop terrace there is an amazing view of the river valley and the distant Contraviesa *sierra*. The bedrooms are simply decorated but they are quiet and clean. The nicest are the ten rooms with their own private terraces, recently grafted to the La Fragua's exisiting rooms. Breakfasts and other meals are served at the sister restaurant of the same name, just 50 metres down the street. It has a cosy pine-clad dining room which has been hoisted above the bar, with windows to three sides that catch that same wonderful view out across the village. La Fragua's menu focuses on things traditional. Try the *cordero a la moruña* (spicy lamb), the *perdíz del cura a la antigua* (partridge) or the generously priced set menu. A friendly and reliable place to stay.

To see and do: visit to a *secadero* where cured hams are prepared, trout-fishing in the Río Trevélez (early May to early September) and walking

HOTEL LOS BÉRCHULES

MAP: 6

Ctra de Bérchules 20
18451 Bérchules

Tel: 958 852530 **Fax:** 958 769000

e-mail: hot.berchules@interbook.net

Web Page: www.berchules.com

Closed: Never

Bedrooms: 4 Singles, 10 Twins and 1 Apartment

Price: Single €30, Twin €40, Apartment €350 per week
including VAT

Meals: Breakfast €3.50, Lunch €7.50 including wine,
Dinner €15 including wine

Getting there: From Málaga take the N-340 to Motril. Just past
Motril turn left to Albuñol and shortly past the village, turn right on
the GR-433 to Cadiar. Here follow the signs for Mecina then turn left
to Bérchules. The hotel is at the bottom of the village on the left.

Management: Alejandro Tamborero

Bérchules is one of the lesser known villages of the Alpujarras. Surrounded by chestnut forests and terraces, irrigated by fast-flowing water channels, its cool mountain air means that this is perfect ham-curing terrain. The hiking round here is magnificent (the GR-7 path loops through the village) and Hotel Los Bérchules is a great first choice for walkers and non-walkers alike. Alejandro and his English mother Wendy greet their guests in a genuine, unaffected manner. There's nothing grand about their simple three-storey hotel but the bedrooms are all that you need and more. They all have twin beds with pine furniture and French windows that lead out to terraces overlooking the valley. Bright, Alpujarra-weave blankets and curtains add a welcome splash of colour. The same fabric brightens the cosy bar-cum-lounge on the ground floor where there's a collection of books about the area and a few novels. Across the way is a similarly snug-feeling dining room. The food is good, the set menu excellent value and Wendy is accustomed to vegetarians and their ways. Her wines are also very honestly priced.

To see and do: visit to a *secadero* where cured hams are prepared and to wine bodegas, walking, and horse-riding

CASA RURAL LAS CHIMENEAS

MAP: 6

Calle Amargura 6
18493 Mairena

Tel: 958 760352 **Fax:** 958 760004

e-mail: dillsley@moebius.es

Web Page: www.moebius.es/contourlines

Closed: Never

Bedrooms: 2 Doubles and 1 Twin in main house,
2 Studio-Apartments and 1 house with 2 Doubles

Price: Double/Twin/Apartment €60 including breakfast VAT

Meals: Breakfast incl. in Double/Twin price but not apartment price,
Packed Lunches €4, Dinner €15 excluding wine

Getting there: From Granada take the A-92 east towards Almería.
After passing Guadix exit for La Calahorra then take the pass of 'El
Puerto de la Ragua' to Laroles. Here, go right to Mairena. Take the
second right into the village and park in the square. Las Chimeneas is
just 30m off the south-east corner of the square.

Management: Emma & David Illsley

David and Emma lived and worked in many different parts of Europe before heading for the Alpujarras, a decision which was inspired in part by English author Gerald Brennan's writings about the area. They arrived in the right place at just the right time. An architect who had completely restored this old village house had decided to move on. It's easy to see why they fell in love with the house and the village. Mairena is beyond the day-trippers shadow at the eastern end of the Alpujarra, a quiet, friendly village "where mules still outnumber cars". The village looks out across deep *barrancos* (gorges) to the distant Contraviesa mountains. The atmosphere that the whole house seems to breathe is one of wholesome, uncluttered simplicity. There is a high-ceilinged guest lounge/diner with a hearth, books, and rocking chairs. Light streams in from its south-facing windows. The bedrooms are every bit as attractive and most are large. Some have terraces and all have wonderful old floors and antique furniture. Many of the guests at Las Chimeneas come to explore the mountains surrounding the village and the Illsleys know all of its loveliest pathways.

To see and do: walking (high peaks of 8000 feet easily accessible), horse-riding, visits to other little-known villages such as Júbar

REFUGIO DE NEVADA

MAP: 6

Ctra de Mairena
18493 Laroles

Tel: 958 760320 or 958 760304 **Fax:** 958 760338

Web Page: www.ctv.es/alpujarr

Closed: Never

Bedrooms: 2 Doubles, 3 Twins and 7 Studios

Price: Double/Twin €36-43, Studio €56 + 7% VAT

Meals: Breakfast €4, Lunch/Dinner €10 including wine

Getting there: From Granada take the A-92 eastwards. Shortly past Guadix, turn right and go over the high 'El Puerto de La Ragua' pass and continue to Laroles. The hotel is on the right as you enter the village.

Management: Eloisa Roman

Laroles lies at the very eastern end of the Alpujarras. You drop down to the village after following the snaking road that leads up and over the spectacular pass of La Ragua. There is wonderful walking and cross-country skiing here when the snows are down. Another good reason for visiting the area is to stay at the Refugio de Nevada. This immensely attractive small hotel is less than a decade old but looks much older thanks to its architect having faithfully followed the dictates of the local architectural lore. Its wooden doors, beams and balconies, slate walls and flat roofs of local *pizarra* slate all feel authentically *alpujarreño*. And you know that you've come to the right place when you're greeted by the warm-hearted, gregarious Eloisa who officiates in the Refugio's cosy little restaurant. The set menu (genuine *comida casera*) changes daily with a lot of the ingredients fresh from husband Manolo's vegetable patch. The bedrooms are just as snug and welcoming as the rest of the hotel. The studios have their own small lounge.

To see and do: horse-riding, walking, visits to other villages of the Alpujarras

JAÉN
PROVINCE

HOTELS 116 TO 120

El Pantono del Tranco

HOSPEDERÍA FUENTENUEVA

MAP: 5

Paseo Arca del Agua s/n
23440 Baeza

Tel: 953 743100 **Fax:** 953 743200

e-mail: fuentenueva@fuentenueva.com

Web Page: www.fuentenueva.com

Closed: Never

Bedrooms: 3 Doubles and 9 Twins

Price: Double/Twin €66-72 + 7% VAT

Meals: Breakfast included, Lunch/Dinner €11 including wine

Getting there: From Granada take the N-323 north towards Madrid/Jaén. Just before Jaén branch right on the N-321 to Baeza. Exit for Baeza, and head all the way through the town centre (where you will pick up signs for Úbeda). The hotel is on the left as you leave the town.

Management: Juan Ramón Orcera

Be honest. When was the last time that you went to prison? There can be few places quite as special as Fuentenueva for "doing time". This small hotel occupies, as you'll have guessed, what once was the town prison for women. It was given a new destiny after the local council gave it a thorough face-lift and entrusted its management to a team of five young folk from the town. Thanks to buckets of youthful enthusiasm and creativity, they have already helped to create a truly original place to stay. Downstairs is an airy entrance hall with a ceramic tiled fountain and a bar and restaurant to either side. All of it is decorated in pastel colours and there is modern art hung in every last corner. Fuentenueva doubles as a gallery where local artists can exhibit their work. The same love of colour is evident in the bedrooms which have bright washes, stencilling and ragged-and-sponged paint finishes. Gaily coloured fabrics add a further dash of razzmatazz. The Hospedería is a hotel with a light heart and beautiful, Renaissance Baeza is right on your doorstep.

To see and do: Baeza and its Renaissance architecture, Úbeda and its Renaissance architecture, the Cazorla Natural Park

MARIA DE MOLINA

MAP: 5

Plaza del Ayuntamiento
23400 Úbeda

Tel: 953 795356 **Fax:** 953 793694

e-mail: hotelmm@hotel-maria-de-molina.com

Web Page: www.hotel-maria-de-molina.com

Closed: 15 July - 15 August

Bedrooms: 2 Singles, 6 Doubles and 10 Twins

Price: Single €46-52, Standard Double/Twin €71-83.50, Special Double/Twin €92-104 + 7% VAT

Meals: Breakfast included, Lunch/Dinner €16 excluding wine

Getting there: From Granada take the N-323 north towards Madrid/Jaén. Just before Jaén branch right on the N-321 to Úbeda then follow signs for 'Casco Antiguo'. The hotel is next door to the *Ayuntamiento* (town hall), signposted as you reach the centre.

Management: Juan Navarro López

Nothing quite prepares you for the magnificence of Úbeda. The town, adrift in a vast ocean of olive groves, is absolutely bursting with stunning Renaissance architecture. All of this grandeur dates from a time when the town's merchants grew rich from the textiles that they traded throughout Europe. Times changed and the town became a sleepy backwater. To wander through its streets by night feels like stepping back into a different age. But María de Molina happily spans the gulf between time past and present. This is the only three-story *palacete* (grand mansion house) in town and the building's joy is its beautifully proportioned courtyard with a splendid double tier of marble columns. In other parts of the hotel, it's hard to believe that you are really sleeping in a 400-year old building. The bedrooms have the comfort, feel and fittings of a five-star hotel and the two dining rooms retain few of their original features. What makes the place memorable is the friendliness of the staff, and, of course, the joy of wandering the surprsingly elegant backstreets of this wonderful old town.

To see and do: Úbeda and its Renaissance architecture, Baeza and its Renaissance architecture, the Cazorla Natural Park

MOLINO LA FARRAGA

MAP: 7

Calle Camino de la Hoz s/n
Apartado de Correos 1
23470 Cazorla

Tel: 953 721249 or 610 737661 **Fax:** 953 721249

e-mail: farraga@teleline.es

Web Page: www.molinolafarraga.com

Closed: 15 December - 28 February

Bedrooms: 1 Single, 3 Doubles, 3 Twins and 2 Suites

Price: Single €40, Double/Twin €60, Suite €96 + 7% VAT

Meals: Breakfast included

Getting there: In Cazorla follow signs for *Ruinas de Santa María* (very narrow streets!). At the far side of the Plaza de Santa María take the road leading between a ruined church and the 'Cueva' restaurant, signposted 'Castillo'. Park on the left by the sign for La Farraga, then cross the bridge and continue on foot for 100m to La Farraga.

Management: Encarni Lopez

You reach Cazorla by way of a vast sea of olive groves. After this seemingly endless monoculture, it comes as a relief to see a rugged mountain crest rising up in the distance. Here, standing sentinel to the *sierra* you catch sight of Cazorla, a white town that clings to its steep eastern flank. The prettiest part of the town is a delightful small square by the ruined church of Santa María. just up the valley from here the old mill house of La Farraga must surely be one of the very nicest places to stay in Andalusia. Abandon your car 100 metres before La Farraga, cross a small bridge and then follow a riverside path to the mill. Its wonderfully verdant garden is criss-crossed by water channels, birds sing from amongst the foliage, and housekeeper, Encarni will be there to greet you with the kindest of smiles. Inside the mill house the feel is one of simple, unaffected comfort and well-being. Rooms vary in dimensions, all are beautifully decorated and feel fresh, airy and peaceful. If you're here to walk, Encarni will prepare breakfast, which is as appealing as the house itself.

To see and do: the Cazorla Natural Park, the old town of Cazorla, Úbeda and Baeza and their Renaissance architecture

HOTEL LA FINCA MERCEDES

MAP: 7

Ctra de la Sierra km 1
23476 La Iruela

Tel: 953 721087 **Fax:** 953 720624

e-mail: info@lafincamercedes.com

Web Page: www.lafincamercedes.com

Closed: Never

Bedrooms: 2 Doubles, 5 Twins and 1 Triple.

Price: Double/Twin €36, Triple €39 + 7% VAT

Meals: Breakfast €3, Lunch/Dinner €15 excluding wine

Getting there: From Úbeda take the N-322 towards Albacete, branch onto the A-315, then the A-319 to Cazorla. Here continue up to a large square at the centre of town and turn left at signs for La Iruela. Stay on this road and pass just beneath La Iruela. La Finca Mercedes is on the left after about 1km.

Management: Mercedes Castillo

If you're looking for an inexpensive and cheerful place to lay your head when visiting the wonderful Cazorla Park, you couldn't do better than to book a night or two at this modest hotel. The life and soul of the place is Mercedes Castillo. It's fitting that the hotel should be named after her. I stayed several nights here when researching a walking guide and was made to feel a part of the family. Things here are on a human scale. The bedrooms are average-sized, decorated with simple pine furniture. The nicest of them look out across the vast expense of olive groves that lie to the east of Cazorla. They are quiet, comfortable and very warm in the winter months (this part of Andalusia can get very cold). The dining room has the same inviting, snug feel about it. A fire burns in the hearth in the colder months and there are paintings of Cazorla and the sea interspersed with a collection of hunting trophies. Simple, regional dishes are on the menu and Mercedes' two daughters, rather quieter than Mum, will often be there to serve you.

To see and do: the Cazorla Natural Park, the old town of Cazorla, Úbeda and Baeza and their Renaissance architecture

LA MESA SEGUREÑA

MAP: 7

Calle Postigo 2
23379 Segura de la Sierra

Tel: 953 482101 **Fax:** 953 482101

e-mail: lamesaseg@hosteria.net

Web Page: www.lamesadesegura.com

Closed: 8 - 31 January

Bedrooms: 5 Studios and 3 Apartments.

Price: Single Studio €40, Studio with double/twin €48-54, Apartment for 2 €48, Apartment for 2 €60-69, Apartment for 4 €72-84 including VAT

Meals: Breakfast €3, Lunch/Dinner €15-20 including wine. The restaurant is closed Sunday and Monday night.

Getting there: From Jaén take the A-316 and then the N-322 towards Albacete. Exit for Puente de Génave and then follow the A-317 via La Puerta de Segura to Orcera, and to Segura. La Mesa Segureña is signposted as you reach the village centre.

Management: Ana María Solares & Francisco Jiménez Aldehuela

You see Segura de la Sierra from miles away. This, the Cazorla Park's most spectacular village, is built on a rocky crag that rises high above the olive groves and is crowned by its lofty castle. Surprisingly few people visit this part of the Park, yet this beautiful village and the walking here (see Santana's book *Walking in Andalucía*) make a visit a double treat. Be sure to stay at La Mesa Segureña. As the name suggests, this place has a distinct culinary focus. Ana María is an artist and she worked wonders when decorating the restaurant and apartments. The general theme is rustic with a really jazzy feel thanks to her use of warm colours (mostly greens and salmon), the abundance of posters and paintings (many her own creations) and her desire that everything should feel "just so". Given the standard of comfort, the apartments are very reasonably priced, and even more so for a family of four. The restaurant offers regional food with a dash of creativity and there is a really good selection of wine on offer.

To see and do: the village and castle of Segura de la Sierra, walking in the Cazorla Natural Park, visit to one of the only square bullrings in Spain

ALMERÍA PROVINCE

HOTELS 121 TO 126

Mojácar

EL JARDIN DE LOS SUEÑOS

MAP: 8

Parque Natural Cabo de Gata - Níjar
04115 Rodalquilar

Tel: 950 525214 or 669 184118 **Fax:** 950 525214

Web Page: www.parquenatural.com/jardin/

Closed: 7 January - end January

Bedrooms: 6 Doubles

Price: Double €66-76 including VAT

Meals: Breakfast included

Getting there: From the E15/N344 exit for Campohermoso/Las Negras. Go through Campohermoso towards Las Negras then turn right towards Rodalquilar. Here, cross the valley and at the entrance to the village continue towards San José for just 100m. El Jardin de los Sueños is signposted to the left.

Management: Eckhard Kost

The Cabo de Gata Natural Park remains one of Andalusia's best-kept secrets. Although you are just a dozen kilometres from the greenhouse belt, this semi-desert area has some of the loveliest beaches and the most hauntingly beautiful landscapes in Iberia. With great sensitivity and an artist's feel for what 'works' Eckhard has crafted an exceptional series of spaces within his 'garden of dreams'. The creative impulse is nurtured in every corner of the house and garden, from contemplating the changing light on the nearby hillsides, the sound of Baroque music drifting out from the lounge, to the sculptural beauty of the palms, bougainvillea and cacti in the magical gardens which surround the house and pool. The bedrooms are diaphanous, intimate and inspire the same mood of peaceful well-being. CD players take the place of TVs and the prints and paintings of contemporary art are as stimulating as the rest of the place. Given all of the above, it seems natural that breakfast in a sheltered courtyard should be a feast for both the eyes and the palate. This is, without question, one of the most remarkable places to stay in southern Spain, so be sure to book well in advance.

To see and do: ceramic manufacturers in Níjar, walking on the coastal paths, beautiful, little-known beaches

HOTEL FAMILY

MAP: 8

Calle La Lomilla s/n
04149 Agua Amarga

Tel: 950 138014 **Fax:** 950 138070

e-mail: riovall@teleline.es

Web Page: www.sawdays.co.uk

Closed: Never

Bedrooms: 1 Double, 7 Twins and 1 Quadruple

Price: Double/Twin €65-100 including VAT

Meals: Breakfast included, Lunch (weekends only) €16 including wine, Dinner €16 including wine

Getting there: From N-344 take Exit 494 signposted Venta del Pobre/Carboneras. Continue towards Carboneras and then turn right to Agua Amarga. Hotel Family is signposted to the right as you enter the village.

Management: Michèle, Marcos & René Maingnon Salmeron

Agua Amarga is one of the most attractive of Almería's coastal villages. People know about the place and in summer you won't have the beach to yourself. But it's still a great place to kick back. René and Michèle Salmeron first came here on holiday and were so taken by the village that they moved south to open this unassuming little *hostal*. The location is perfect, a couple of hundred metres from the village on the far bank of the (dry) river that cuts down from the hills. The Family's restaurant has become an obligatory stopover for many of the inland ex-pat community when they come for a day by the sea. Michèle cooks well and the huge portions have no hint of nouvelle cuisine. Her specialities include duck *à l'orange*, wild boar and stuffed tomatoes. All meals are accompanied by heaps of good vegetables and taped music (e.g., Elton John). The dining room looks out to the swimming pool, as do the bedrooms. The nicest are those that have recently been built on top of the original edifice. The Family has no airs of grandeur but its rooms are light, clean and comfortable.

To see and do: walking, beaches, the scuba diving school in Agua Amarga, the Cabo de Gata Park, the village of Níjar

FINCA LISTONERO

MAP: 8

Cortijo Grande
04639 Turre

Tel: 950 479094 **Fax:** 950 479094

e-mail: listonero@wanadoo.es

Web Page: www.fincalistonero.com

Closed: Never

Bedrooms: 1 Double and 4 Twins

Price: Double/Twin €75-95 + 7% VAT

Meals: Breakfast included, Lunch - snacks only,
Dinner €30 excluding drinks. Restaurant closed on Sunday nights

Getting there: From the N-340/E-15 take Exit 520 towards
Turre/Mojácar. After 3km turn right into the entrance of Cortijo
Grande. Continue towards Cortijo Cabrera and Listonero is
signposted on the right, after 3.5km.

Management: Graeme Gibson & David Rice

David and Graham might be known to some readers living on the Costa del Sol. They used to run the Yellow Book restaurant in Estepona. After a brief period in Australia, they returned to southern Spain, this time to the mountains of Almería, where they have set up another marvellous restaurant which doubles as a country-house hotel. The food is to write home about. David is in charge of things culinary and his cuisine is gourmet, flavoursome and beautifully presented. Meals tend to begin with an aperitif in Listonero's lounge, which is decorated in soothing cool peppermint and is particularly memorable at night when its several lamps and candles are lit. The mood is romantic, relaxing and intimate. The bedrooms (choose between the pink, yellow, green or blue depending on your mood) are just as appealing and are set around a shaded patio whose salmon pink colour provides a beautiful contrast to all of the greenery. A convivial, house-party atmosphere is guaranteed should you stay at Listonero and there's a wonderful pool sculpted into the mountainside just beneath the house.

To see and do: beaches, walking in the Cabo de Gata Park, the village of Mojácar, Mini Hollywood where spaghetti westerns were filmed

CORTIJO EL NACIMIENTO

MAP: 8

Sierra Cabrera
04639 Turre

Tel: 950 528090

Web Page: www.pagina.de/elnacimiento

Closed: November

Bedrooms: 4 Doubles and 1 Twin

Price: Double/Twin €36 including VAT

Meals: Breakfast included, Dinner €12 including wine

Getting there: From the N-340/E-15 take Exit 520 towards Turre/Mojácar. After 3km turn right into the entrance of Cortijo Grande. Continue towards Cabrera for exactly 4.9km and then turn right onto a dirt road (signposted here).

Management: Adolfo & Maria Valdés

Most people who head up into the Cabrera mountains are bound for Cortijo Grande. This amazing collection of luxurious, hilltop villas was the brainchild of an English architect who also had the whacky idea of converting the gardens of a Moorish palace into two full-sized crown bowling greens! Cortijo El Nacimiento has an altogether different feel. Adolfo and María are a friendly Spanish couple who headed for the hills in search of *'the good life,'* and for the last 11 years have welcomed guests to this 200-year-old rambling farm house. This is the complete antithesis of the chain hotel and might not be to everyone's taste. You swim in a deep pool which was created by damming the river. Bedrooms are reached via creaking stairs where bathrooms might be separated by just a curtain. Vegetarian suppers (many of the ingredients organically grown in María's vegetable garden) are served round one large table where the *lingua franca* may well be Spanish. This is a place with masses of personality and no airs of grandeur, and anybody with vague Eco leanings will love it.

To see and do: walking in the Natural Park of Cabo de Gata, interesting archeaological sites, the villages of Mojácar and Bédar

HOTEL TIKAR

MAP: 8

Ctra Garrucha a Vera s/n
04630 Garrucha

Tel: 950 617131 **Fax:** 950 617132

e-mail: hoteltikar@hoteltikar.com

Web Page: www.hoteltikar.com

Closed: 10 December - 10 January

Bedrooms: 6 Suites

Price: Suite €57-115 + 7% VAT

Meals: Breakfast included, Lunch €15,
Dinner €19.50 excluding wine

Getting there: From the N-340 take Exit 534 for Garrucha.
Continue past Vera and then on round to Garrucha. At the roundabout, continue straight on and the hotel is on your right.

Management: Beatriz Gallego de Lerma & Sean McMahon

Sean, Beatriz and their young sons Diego and Pablo have stamped their personality on this small, modern restaurant and hotel (it's easy to spot its gay blue and white facade as you leave Garrucha) and it is already making big waves amongst the local ex-pat community. The decoration of the lounge and restaurant is a wonderfully orchestrated mix of dark parquet, burnt orange and blue ragged walls, elegant teak chairs and modern art—the hotel doubles as an exhibition space for young artists. The food is just as cosmopolitan, the sort of fare you might get in one of California's cafes—fresh vegetables, light sauces, a high salad content and the best cuts of meat. The wine list is just as interesting, not just *Riojas* and *Riberas* but also good bottles from Chile, Argentina, South Africa and France. And although this is, to quote Sean, "a restaurant with rooms," you'll stay in a large, beautifully designed and decorated bedroom whose level of comfort is amazing given the price. Beatriz and Sean are the nicest hosts and, believe me, theirs is one of the most special small hotels around.

To see and do: colourful evening fish auction in Garrucha, the beaches of Vera and Garrucha, the Cabo de Gata Natural Park

LOS SIBILEYS

MAP: 8

Nogalte 84
Puerto Lumbreras
30800 Lorca

Tel: 968 439024 **Fax:** 968 439024

Closed: Never

Bedrooms: 2 Doubles and 2 Twins

Price: Double/Twin €70 including VAT

Meals: Breakfast included, Lunch - tapas/snacks €9.50,
Dinner €21 including wine

Getting there: From P. Lumbreras go west on the N-342 then take
Exit 93 for Henares. At a small roundabout take the second exit for
Servicios. Pass the petrol station and after 1.5km go left over the
motorway to a roundabout. Here take last exit and after 100m, turn
right at the sign Camino de la Venta de la Petra a Nogalte. Take the
3km track to house.

Management: Judith & Karl Lanchbury

Right on the easternmost border of Andalusia is Hacienda de Los Sibileys, an isolated farmhouse in the midst of an amazing multi-coloured landscape of ochre, terracotta and burned sienna, all of it softened and brought to life by groves of olive and almonds. It's easy to see why the area is attracting more and more ex-pats in search of their Arcadia-in-the-sun. The Lanchburys were amongst the first to arrive and they chose a blissfully isolated, tranquil spot on which to build their small guest house. Things have been built on a generous scale at Los Sibileys. The guest rooms are big with attractive Mexican-style furniture and the most comfortable of beds. The same spacious feel is apparent in the lounge and dining room where there are several prints and oils with a nautical theme (Karl chartered yachts for many years). Judith will happily prepare you a light *tapas* lunch if you are tempted to laze by the pool. I thoroughly enjoyed Judith's cooking, Karl's choice of wine, and the kindness of them both.

To see and do: horse-riding, ornithology, the Saturday market in Vélez Rubio, the Moorish castle and Letreros cave (with paleaolithic art) in Vélez Rubio

GLOSSARY

albero	a deep ochre colour—that of the sand in the bullring
añil	a light blue colour with a hint of purple
barranco	a deep sided gorge, typical of La Alpujarra
chocolate	hot chocolate, essential to accompany 'churros'
churros	long, thin do-nuts, best accompanied by 'chocolate'
cortijo	a farm: can be large, medium-sized or small
degustación	a tasting – of wine, cheese, olive oil etc
fino	dry sherry
hammam	arabic term for a bath house
hostal	a simple inn
huerta	an irrigated plot of land or allotment
judería	the Jewish quarter
kilim	a rug from the Middle East
latifundio	a very large estate
levante	a hot, dry wind that blows hard from the East
lomo	loin (nearly always of pork)
manzanilla	similar to *fino* but from the area round Sanlúcar
matanza	the slaughter and preparation of a pig
mudéjar	Moorish style of architecture but post-conquest
palacete	a grand town or country mansion house
posada	a small village/country hotel (orig. coaching inn)
rejas	wrought-iron window/door grille
tapa	a small plate of food served with an apéritif

USEFUL PHONE NUMBERS

Almería	Tourist office	950 274355
	Guardía Civil	950 256122
Cádiz	Tourist office	956 211313
	Guardía Civil	956 253370
Córdoba	Tourist office	957 200522
	Guardía Civil	957 414800
Granada	Tourist office	958 225990
	Guardía Civil	958 185400
	Alhambra (tickets)	902 224460
Huelva	Tourist office	959 257403
	Guardía Civil	959 241900
Jaén	Tourist office	953 222737
	Guardía Civil	953 250340
Málaga	Tourist office	95 2213445
	Guardía Civil	95 2071520
	Picasso Museum	902 443377
	Airport	952 048804
Sevilla	Tourist office	95 4221404
	Guardía Civil	95 4231902
Emergencies		112
Renfe		902 240202
Weather Info (in Spanish)		906 365329
Directory Enquiries		11818
International Enquiries		11825
Alarm Service		096

INDEX BY HOTEL NAME

HOTEL NAME	PLACE	HOTEL NUMBER
Hostal El Anón	Jimena de la Frontera	044
Hostal Marbella	Fuengirola	076
Hostal Seneca	Córdoba	097
Hostal Suecia	Granada	102
Hostería del Laurel	Sevilla	016
Hurricane, Hotel	Tarifa	039
La Almuña	Gaucín	063
La Bobadilla, Hotel	Loja	100
La Carmela	Vejer de la Frontera	032
La Cartuja de Cazalla	Cazalla de la Sierra	010
La Casa del Califa	Vejer de la Frontera	034
La Casa Grande	Arcos de la Frontera	029
La Cazalla	Ronda	056
La Era, Hotel	Casarabonela	079
La Finca Mercedes, Hotel	La Iruela	119
La Fragua, Hotel	Trevélez	112
La Fructuosa	Gaucín	060
La Fuente de la Higuera	Ronda	051
La Hormiga Voladora	Bolonia Tarifa	036
La Hostería de Don José	Ojén	072
La Mesa Segureña	Segura de la Sierra	120
La Peña, Hotel	Tarifa	040
La Posada del Angel	Ojén	071
La Posada del Conde	Ardales	080
La Posada del Torcal	Villanueva de la Concepción	083
La Posada Morisca	Frigiliana	091
La Tartana	La Herradura	109
Larios, Hotel	Málaga	086
Las Casas de la Juderia	Sevilla	018
Las Islas	Fuengirola	077
Las Navezuelas	Cazalla de la Sierra	011
Los Bérchules, Hotel	Bérchules	113

INDEX BY PLACE

PLACE	HOTEL NAME	HOTEL NUMBER
Córdoba	Hotel Amistad	096
Córdoba	Hostal Seneca	097
El Burgo	Hotel Posada del Canónigo	069
El Rocío	Hotel Toruño	007
Estación de Cortes	El Gecko	058
Frigiliana	Hotel Rural Los Caracoles	090
Frigiliana	La Posada Morisca	091
Fuengirola	Las Islas	077
Fuengirola	Hostal Marbella	076
Garrucha	Hotel Tikar	126
Gaucín	Hotel Casablanca	061
Gaucín	La Almuña	063
Gaucín	Cortijo El Puerto del Negro	064
Gaucín	La Fructuosa	060
Gaucín	El Nobo	062
Gaucín	Hacienda La Herriza	065
Granada	Palacio de Santa Inés	101
Granada	Hostal Suecia	102
Granada	Hotel Carmen de Santa Inés	103
Granada	Hotel America	104
Granada	Hotel Casa Morisca	105
Granada	Casa del Capitel Nazarí	106
Granada	Casa del Aljarife	107
Grazalema	Hostal Casa de las Piedras	046
Guaro	El Molino Santisteban	078
Guillena	Hotel Cortijo Aguila Real	012
Jabugo	Finca la Silladilla	001
Jimena de la Frontera	Hostal El Anón	044
Jimena de la Frontera	Posada La Casa Grande	045
La Herradura	La Tartana	109
La Iruela	Hotel La Finca Mercedes	119
Laroles	Refugio de Nevada	115
Las Cabezas de San Juan	Hacienda de San Rafael	022
Las Cabezas de San Juan	Alguaciles Bajos	021
Loja	Hotel La Bobadilla	100

PLACE	HOTEL NAME	HOTEL NUMBER
Lorca	Los Sibileys	127
Mairena	Casa Rural Las Chimeneas	114
Málaga	Hotel Larios	086
Málaga	Hotel Cortijo La Reina	087
Maro	Hotel Romantico Casa Maro	093
Mecina Fondales	Hotel Albergue de Mecina	110
Mijas	Hacienda de San José	074
Mijas Costa	The Beach House	075
Montecorto	El Tejar	049
Nerja	Hotel Paraíso del Mar	092
Ojén	La Posada del Angel	071
Ojén	La Hostería de Don José	072
Osuna	Hotel Palacio M. de la Gomera	020
Palma del Río	Hospedería de San Francisco	094
Priego de Córdoba	Posada Real	099
Riogordo	Hospedería Retamar	088
Rodalquilar	El Jardín de los Sueños	121
Ronda	Alavera de los Baños	054
Ronda	La Fuente de la Higuera	051
Ronda	Hotel San Gabriel	055
Ronda	Cortijo Puerto Llano	048
Ronda	El Horcajo	047
Ronda	La Cazalla	056
Ronda	Finca La Guzmana	053
Ronda	Arriadh Hotel	052
Ronda	Cortijo Las Piletas	050
Sabinillas	Cortijo la Vizcaronda	067
San Martín del Tesorillo	Cortijo El Papudo	066
San Roque	Hostal Atrium San Roque	042
Sanlúcar de Barrameda	Los Helechos	023
Sanlúcar de Barrameda	Posada de Palacio	024
Segura de la Sierra	La Mesa Segureña	120
Sevilla	Hotel Simón	015
Sevilla	Casa Nº 7	014
Sevilla	Hostería del Laurel	016

YOUR OPINIONS

Please let us know about your experiences at the places that we include in this book. And please let us know about any good places you discover which you think merit an entry in the next edition.

NAME of HOTEL: _____

Date of visit: _____

Your comments:

_____

_____

_____

_____

_____

Your opinion of the food & wine:

_____

_____

_____

Your name: _____

Address: _____

_____

_____

_____

Contact number: _____

(if you are happy to give us these details).

Please send by post to   Guy Hunter-Watts
El Tejar
29430 Montecorto, Málaga,
by fax to: (00 34) 95 2184053
or by e-mail to guyhw@mercuryin.es

Many thanks.